BEET THIS

xxxxxxxx

An Unofficial
Schrute Farms Cookbook

Tyanni Niles
Sam Kaplan
Keith Riegert

Published in the US by:
ULYSSES PRESS
PO Box 3440
Berkeley, CA 94703
www.ulyssespress.com

ISBN: 978-1-64604-188-6
Library of Congress Control Number: 2021931327

Printed in the United States by Versa Press
10 9 8 7 6 5 4 3 2 1

Managing editor: Claire Chun
Project editor: Renee Rutledge
Editor: Phyllis Elving
Front cover design: Amy King
Interior design and layout: what!design @ whatweb.com
Production assistant: Yesenia Garcia-Lopez
Interior photographs: shutterstock.com except page 5 by Keith Riegert
    and pages 11, 16, 20, 32, 36, 46, 52, 60, 62, 64, 66, 72, 78, 82, 84, 94, 100,
    103, 106, 108, 116, 122, 132, and 139 by Monkeyscratch

NOTE TO READERS: This book is an independent and unauthorized fan publication. No endorsement, license, sponsorship, or affiliation with *The Office*, NBC, Deedle-Dee Productions, 3 Arts Entertainment, Reveille Productions, Shine America, Universal Media Studios, Universal Television, or other copyright or trademark holders is claimed or suggested. All references in this book to copyrighted or trademarked characters and other elements of *The Office* television show are the property of their respective owners and used for informational purposes only. All trademarked products that appear in the book are the property of their respective owners and used for informational purposes only. The authors and publisher encourage readers to watch, rent, purchase, and support *The Office* television show, and to patronize the quality brands mentioned in this book.

TABLE OF CONTENTS

MAINS 69

SWEETS 119

DRINKS 131

FOREWORD

The Office holds a very special place in our hearts. Michael, Dwight, Pam, Jim, and Darryl helped us get through post-college doldrums, graduate school, breakups and marriages, raising small humans, and—as we are writing this—the most ridiculously awful global pandemic in more than a century. Suffice it to say, we're really big fans.

After years of thinking about it, we finally summoned the courage to write this book—a parody and homage to Dwight Schrute and his family's rich history as the purveyors of Schrute Farms, the most respected and storied beet farm in Honesdale, Pennsylvania. To get started, we asked ourselves one main question: What would a family cookbook look like if the Schrute family passed recipes down from one generation to the next, and then the next? Heavy on the beets, Pennsylvania Dutch cuisine, and classic German recipes, the cookbook you hold in your hands is what we imagine our favorite quirky, stoic, and self-sufficient family would have compiled over the decades.

So, chop up a couple of ruby queens, dust off your Le Creuset Dutch ovens, and join us on a culinary road trip to the manure-laden beet fields outside Scranton, PA.

Genießen (enjoy),
Tyanni Niles
Sam Kaplan
Keith Riegert

INTRODUCTION: BEET THAT, IDIOT

Fact: The beet is the most superior plant-based food ever discovered by man. If edible plants were to be given belts to denote rank and superiority, the beet would be a seventh-degree black belt. Beetroot is literally packed with iron, vitamin C, potassium, manganese, folate, protein, phosphorus, and enough dietary fiber to keep you regular well into your hundreds. In addition, the regular consumption of beets has been associated with health benefits such as boosted all-around stamina, improved circulation, lower blood pressure, and enhanced, jaguar-like reflexes. Enjoy this cookbook as if your life depends on it. It does.

All competent historians believe domestication of the beet allowed early civilization to flourish around 2000 BCE thanks to its versatility.

BEET FARMING 101

So, you want to become a beet farmer. Fantastic! The first thing to know is that you will inevitably fail. Proper beet farming requires an incredibly varied skill set, which you likely do not have. Here are just a *few* of the skills required to farm beets:

1. The strength of at least one grown adult human and one adolescent human.

2. Nothing lower than a green belt in karate.

3. Facility with weapons (often referred to as "gardening tools").

4. Access to excellent soil.

5. A beginner's knowledge of both pest control and mind control.

Soil: Beets are like babies. They grow best when planted in tilled, slightly moist soil chock-full of organic matter (invest in plenty of manure). The optimum soil acidity is a pH of 6.4 (identical to healthy urine).

The typical life of a beet over three months.

BEET THIS

Temperature: There's a reason that Northeastern Pennsylvania is known as the "beet basket of the world"—beets grow best in cool temperatures, ideally between 50° and 65°F (283° and 291.5° Kelvin). You'll want to hit pause on planting when temperatures climb into the 80s (300s).

Sowing: Plant your beet seeds a fortnight ahead of spring's final frost.[1] Sow each small handful of seeds 1 inch deep and 6 inches apart (in rows spaced a foot apart). Your average healthy acre should yield about 18 tons of beets—enough to feed a Schrute family of four for nearly a week.

Nurturing: Beets thrive in slightly moist soil. Consistently water throughout the growing season to avoid letting the soil dry out. You can grow superior beets in both full and partial sun.

Remove weeds by hand to ensure the beets aren't disturbed. To guard against potential pests—such as slugs, weevils, and leaf miners—we strongly recommend assigning a small child the honor of Overnight Guard Duty.

Harvesting: Your beets will be ready for harvesting between 40 (for baby beets) and 80 days (fully grown beets) after planting. Take the same care when digging out each beetroot that you would in helping to remove a young foal from the birth canal.

Storing: You can store your harvested beets in your refrigerator for up to 3 weeks. Beet greens can stay fresh and crisp up to a week in the refrigerator in a plastic bag.

---

1 For the most accurate information about weather, we recommend the *Schrute Family Farmer's Almanac*, now in its 250th edition.

A BEET-WORTHY KITCHEN

Choosing the right beets will make or break your dish. If you ever come across a couple of beets, do whatever you want with them. Fry them, sauté them, whatever. We already know what to do with ours. But as much as we'd love for you to figure it out yourself, our editors recommended we let you in on our family secrets. So, here are our tips:

Selecting: Superior beets are vibrant in color and firm and round. There are many beet varieties out there (e.g., red, golden, Chioggia, you name it!), but for the sake of this cookbook, we will be using the classic red beet. When choosing your red beets, look for a deep red color. The skin should be unblemished. If the leaves are attached, they should be a bright green. Red beets have a rich, earthy flavor but will gain a bit of sweetness the longer they are stored.

Cleaning: Twist or trim the stems and leaves of your beets to about ½ inch. The great thing about beets? They're not just for roasting. Repurpose the leaves and use them to make other delicious recipes like salads or Beet Green Chips (page 38). Lightly scrub the beets under cold water with a clean brush or rough sponge to remove dirt and debris. Don't worry too much about the dirt in the stems; you can remove them with a knife by cutting right below the dark area near the top of the root.

Superior varieties of beets include (from left to right) the ringed Chioggia, white Avalanche, sweet Golden, and virile Schrute.

Peeling: Leaving the skins on helps retain the flavor and the color of the beets. If you are baking or roasting, then it's best to leave the skin on. Peeling beets can be a messy job, so you'll want to cover your work area with plastic wrap and wear gloves if you don't want stained hands. For raw beets, use a peeler like you would use on a potato. For cooked beets, rub the skin off with a paper towel or under running water with your hands.

Boiling: Bring a large pot of water to boil. Add about 1 tablespoon of salt to the pot. Clean the beets and trim the leaves. Place the beets in the water and cover the pot. Let simmer for 20 to 40 minutes depending on the size. (Small beets take about 20 minutes to boil, medium beets about 30 minutes, and large beets about 40 minutes.) Remove from the water and let cool.

Testing for Doneness: Before you peel your beets after they've finished boiling, you'll want to insert a knife into the center of the beet. If a fork can easily pierce it, then it is ready.

BEET THIS

BREAKFAST

Beets for breakfast? Yes, loser. Schrutes have been consuming at least two medium beets per person before 4:30 a.m. for as long as there have been horses to milk. As a rule of thumb, a proper breakfast should pack enough protein, carbs, fat, and vitamins to power you through 5 acres of seed-sowing without doubling over from hunger pangs. The recipes in this chapter are geared toward getting your day off to a sprinting start.

ONE RAW BEET

The real potency of beets comes from their betanin, the pigment that gives beets their crimson color. Most people know that betanin is a powerful antimicrobial agent. What is less known is that betanin has been proven to alter the color of skin. When eaten in large enough doses (four or five beets daily), beet betanin will give your human cheek a soft crimson glow. This will give you a trustworthy face. Then people will tell you their secrets. And then you will have power over them.

Serves 1 〡 Prep time: 1 minute

1 beet

Stroll to your beet field, remove a healthy beet from the ground, wash it, enjoy.

BEET BISCUITS WITH RABBIT GRAVY

Looking for a breakfast treat that is sure to remind you of carefree childhood days? Look no further than this comforting recipe for hot beet biscuits smothered in rich rabbit gravy—just the way *Großvater* used to make.

Serves 3 or 4 ⏐ Prep time: 10 minutes ⏐ Cook time: 20 to 25 minutes

BEET BISCUITS

2 cups all-purpose flour

1 tablespoon baking powder

1 teaspoon salt

1 stick (4 ounces) unsalted butter, melted

½ cup buttermilk

2 medium beets, roasted, peeled, and puréed (see Whole Roasted Beets, page 53)

1 teaspoon sugar

1. Preheat the oven to 400°F.

2. In a medium bowl, thoroughly blend the flour, baking powder, and salt. Slowly mix in the melted butter.

3. In a separate medium bowl, use a spoon to mix together the buttermilk and puréed beets until creamy; add to the dry ingredients and combine well.

4. Remove the dough onto a floured surface and gently knead. Shape into about 8 to 10 balls, then pat the dough balls into flat rounds about 1 inch tall.

5. Refrigerate the dough balls until the rabbit gravy (below) is 10 minutes from completion. Then bake for 15 minutes, or until lightly browned; smother with the rabbit gravy and serve hot.

1 rabbit, deboned

1 medium onion, chopped

1 stick (4 ounces) unsalted butter

3 heads garlic, diced

1 tablespoon all-purpose flour

2 cups milk (can be nondairy) or rabbit broth

6 ounces cream cheese

1 teaspoon salt

1 teaspoon black pepper, to taste

1. Mince the rabbit meat, making sure to remove any bones.

2. In a large skillet, sauté the onion in half of the stick of butter over medium-high heat for 2 minutes, then add the diced garlic and cook for 1 more minute. Add the rabbit meat and the remaining butter.

3. Slowly stir in the flour and cook for 2 to 3 minutes over medium-high heat. Gradually add the milk or rabbit broth and cook, stirring, for about 3 minutes or until the sauce thickens.

4. Spoon in the block of cream cheese, salt, and pepper. Continue to cook, stirring occasionally, until the gravy reaches the desired consistency.

BEET THIS

SHREDDED BEET PORRIDGE WITH SOWN WILD OATS

Many of you are probably feeding your children some version of processed wheat or sugared garbage for breakfast. But if you want them to grow up with unbreakable bones and the strength of a full-grown wolf plus a wolfling pup, switch immediately to this nutritious breakfast dish.

Serves 2 ⫸ Prep time: 2 minutes ⫸ Cook time: 5 to 15 minutes

1 small beet, peeled

1 red-skinned apple

1 cup wild oats, dried

2 cups oat milk

1 tablespoon ground cinnamon

1 tablespoon brown sugar

1 tablespoon coconut oil

halved or slivered nuts and other toppings, as desired

1. Grate the beet and the apple into a medium bowl, then transfer to a small saucepan.

2. Add the remaining ingredients and simmer over medium heat for 5 to 15 minutes, until the desired consistency is achieved.

3. To serve, sprinkle the nuts on top along with any other toppings of your choosing.

NO-BAKE BEET BAR

These hearty, semisweet beet bars come to us from Grandaunt Petra, who spent a week trapped beneath an overturned tractor with nothing more than a burlap sack of bars and a gallon jug of warm horse milk. By the time she was freed, she'd put on 4 pounds of lean muscle.

Makes 12 bars ‖ Prep time: 10 minutes

1 medium boiled beet, peeled and roughly chopped

1 cup pitted dates

½ cup dried pumpkin seeds

½ cup shredded coconut

2 cups old-fashioned rolled oats

½ cup chopped walnuts

1 teaspoon ground cinnamon

½ teaspoon salt

½ cup almond butter

3½ ounces semisweet chocolate, divided

1. Add the beets and dates to a food processor and process for 1 minute; set aside.

2. In a large bowl, mix the pumpkin seeds, coconut, oats, walnuts, cinnamon, and salt. Set aside.

3. Heat the almond butter in a small pan over low heat just until it melts.

4. Add the melted almond butter and the beet mixture to the pumpkin-seed mixture. Use a wooden spoon or your hands to mix everything together.

5. Chop half the chocolate into small chunks and add to the pumpkin-seed mixture, stirring to combine.

6. Line a 9 x 13-inch baking pan with parchment paper or coat with cooking spray. Press the beet mixture into the prepared pan, using your hands or a spatula to pack it in very firmly.

7. Place the remainder of the chocolate in a small, microwave-safe dish and melt in the microwave for 30 seconds. Drizzle the melted chocolate over the beet bars. Cover the pan with plastic wrap and refrigerate for a couple of hours.

8. With a sharp knife, cut the cooled mixture into 12 bars. Leftovers will keep for a week in an airtight container placed in the refrigerator.

Cook's Note: Feel free to switch the walnuts for almonds, or the cinnamon for nutmeg or allspice.

AUNT GERTRUDE'S BEET GRUEL

A warm bowl of beet porridge is an ideal way to start the day, and no other beet gruel can compare to Auntie Gertrude's Beet Gruel. The health benefits of this Schrute family staple include lowered cholesterol, increased energy, and the ability to hold your breath twice as long as the average human.

Serves 2 | Prep time: 5 minutes | Cook time: 18 to 24 minutes

1 medium beet, peeled and diced

1 cup milk (can be nondairy)

½ cup old-fashioned rolled oats

1 apple, sliced and diced

1 teaspoon unsalted butter

1 to 2 teaspoons honey

1 teaspoon ground cinnamon

1 teaspoon ground ginger

toppings: walnuts, pecans, slivered almonds, dried bear meat (optional)

1. Place the diced beet in a small saucepan over high heat with enough water to fully cover; bring to a boil. Reduce heat to medium-low and let simmer for 15 to 20 minutes, stirring occasionally, until the beet pieces are tender. Remove from heat and drain off the water.

2. In a small saucepan over medium heat, bring the milk to a slow simmer. Stir in the oats. Add the diced beet and apple and let simmer, stirring occasionally, for 3 to 4 minutes or until the oats have softened and thickened. (Note: If you prefer a softer mouth feel, add more milk and cook for a few more minutes.)

3. Stir in the butter, honey, cinnamon, and ginger. Add toppings to your taste and serve immediately.

SALADS

In America, salads have been unduly maligned as "wimpy" and "rabbit food." But the titanosaurus only ate salads, and it was the size of 12 African elephants. And rabbits make love thousands of times each year. Now who's wimpy, wimp?

PICKLED BEET ENGLISH SALAD

Although we normally don't recommend anything as exotic as British cuisine, their pickled beet salad makes a surprisingly refreshing snack. If you have no other option, use chicken eggs, but the flavorful eggs of either the rough-legged hawk or the snowy owl will turn this dish from delicious to downright *köstlich*.

Serves 2 to 4 ⬩ Prep time: 10 to 15 minutes

2 heads romaine lettuce (or another kind if you prefer)

⅓ cup minced watercress

2 stalks celery, finely sliced

2 tablespoons chopped mint leaves

salt and black pepper, to taste

dash of sugar

1 lemon

olive oil or salad dressing (optional)

2 or 3 hard-boiled eggs, sliced

2 Beet Pickles, sliced (page 47)

1. Pick (if you've grown your own), wash, and drain the lettuce, then break into pieces.

2. Toss the lettuce, watercress, celery, and mint in a large salad bowl. Sprinkle with salt, pepper, and sugar before squeezing lemon juice evenly over the salad.

3. If you like, add olive oil or a salad dressing of your choice. Garnish with slices of hard-boiled eggs and pickled beets.

DUTCH HERRING SALAD WITH BEETS

This robust Dutch dish is packed with all the protein and nutrients you would need to cross the Atlantic by rowboat. Combining tangy brined herring with a smorgasbord of other ingredients, Dutch salads are indisputably among the great Dutch exports, surpassed only by the pendulum clock, the atlas, and of course, the new astrolabe—invented by a family hero, Dutch geographer Gemma Frisius.

Serves 2 to 4 | Prep time: 10 to 15 minutes

4 Dutch herring, heads and tails removed and cut into small pieces

1 tart apple, finely chopped

1 small yellow onion, finely chopped

8 small sweet and sour gherkins, finely chopped

2 hard-boiled eggs, finely chopped

½ cup shredded carrots

1 pound beets, boiled, peeled, and cubed

1 pound waxy potatoes, boiled, peeled, and cubed

1 cup olive oil

1 cup mayonnaise

1 tablespoon apple cider vinegar

salt, to taste

black pepper, to taste

½ head Boston lettuce, for serving (optional)

1. In a large bowl, combine the herring, apple, onion, gherkins, eggs, carrots, beets, and potatoes.

2. Make a dressing by whisking together the olive oil, mayonnaise, vinegar, salt, and pepper.

3. Pour the dressing over the salad mixture and stir until well combined. Serve on lettuce leaves, if desired.

Cook's Note: You can purchase Dutch herring online at www.thedutchstore.com and www.mercato.com.

SWISS BEET SALAD

Beet farming is an imperfect science, and every year you're bound to have some failures. This can happen because you're a loser and planted your beets in overly acidic soil. Or maybe you had a weevil attack or a leaf miner infestation, leaving your beets shriveled and emasculated. Enough with the misery. Because of the robust spice blend in this classic salad, it is an ideal way to utilize beets that might otherwise be unacceptable. To bring out the tang of the vinegar and the aromatic clove flavors, draw your well water the same day you plan on boiling the beets.

Serves 6 ⎪ Prep time: 10 to 15 minutes, plus overnight to marinate

2 pounds beets, boiled, peeled, and sliced

⅛ cup balsamic vinegar

½ cup olive oil

1 teaspoon whole cloves

2 bay leaves

salt and black pepper, to taste

1 teaspoon sugar (optional)

1. Place the sliced beets in a nonmetallic dish. Bear in mind that plastic might stain, so it's preferable to use ceramic or glass.

2. Whisk together the vinegar and oil, then stir in the cloves, bay leaves, salt and pepper, and sugar (if using).

3. Pour the mixture over the beets and toss gently, being careful not to break the beet slices. Cover with plastic wrap and refrigerate overnight to allow the flavors to develop and intensify. Serve either chilled or at room temperature.

NEAPOLITAN SALAD

They say revenge is a dish best served cold. You know what other dish is best served cold? This one. For an interesting variation, try adding a small dollop of laxative. This allows you to serve two dishes at once to your favorite enemy: cold revenge, and cold Neapolitan Salad. However, if you're enjoying it yourself or with someone you trust, freely swap out the laxative or the capers for crumbled bacon.

Serves 6 ❙ Prep time: 10 minutes ❙ Cook time: 8 minutes

4 boneless, skinless chicken breast halves

2 cups diced boiled beets

1 cup waxy potatoes, boiled, peeled, and diced

½ small red onion, minced

¼ cup mayonnaise

¼ cup sour cream

lemon juice, to taste

1 head romaine lettuce (or another kind if you prefer)

1 hard-boiled egg, minced

1 tablespoon capers

1. In a pan of lightly salted water, simmer the chicken for 8 minutes, or until cooked through.

2. Remove the chicken pieces from the cooking water, let cool, and then cut into 1-inch chunks. Place in a bowl with the beets, potatoes, and onion.

3. In a small bowl, stir the mayonnaise and sour cream together. Add lemon juice to taste. Stir the dressing into the beet mixture.

4. Line a serving bowl or platter with lettuce leaves. Top with the beet salad, then sprinkle with the boiled egg and capers to serve.

SALADS

29

THE BETA-BRASSICA PACT: BEET AND CABBAGE SALAD

What is the single most important ingredient in this salad? There are *two* single most important ingredients in this salad: beets and cabbage. The union between these two vegetables has been likened to history's great alliances, such as the Warsaw Pact, the Triple Entente, and of course, the Last Alliance of Elves and Men.

Serves 4 | Prep time: 1 hour, 10 minutes

1 head savoy cabbage, torn to pieces

4 medium beets, boiled, peeled, and sliced

1 small red onion, finely chopped

salt and black pepper, preferably fresh ground, to taste

1 cup red wine vinegar

¼ cup olive oil

1. Put the cabbage and sliced beets in a medium bowl. Sprinkle in the onion and add salt and pepper to taste.

2. Pour the vinegar over the salad and let stand for an hour. Then drain off the vinegar and add the olive oil. Toss well and serve.

BEET THIS

SNACKS
AND SIDES

For generations, Schrutes have held demanding occupations. From beet farmer, war criminal, and goat herder to Big Foot tracker, outlaw, and time traveler, our jobs have always required ample sustenance. If you are similarly employed, then surely you know the importance of portable snacks and nutritious sides. Here are several.

SCHRUTE JERKY

Looking for a nutritious, rich, chewy meat snack to keep you from that midafternoon lull? Forget your sugar squares and granola rectangles. Break out your liquid smoke instead. Jerky can be made from practically anything, from tame domestic sources such as beef, pork, goat, and pony to more exotic fare such as wild deer, kudu, werewolf, and beaver. This is definitely a recipe you will use over and over again.

Makes 18 strips ⫻ Prep time: 10 minutes, plus overnight to marinate ⫻ Cook time: 4 to 8 hours

2 pounds top round or flank steak

½ cup low-sodium soy sauce

1 teaspoon liquid smoke

1 teaspoon seasoned salt

1 teaspoon onion powder

½ teaspoon garlic powder

2 tablespoons Worcestershire sauce

2 teaspoons black pepper

½ teaspoon chili pepper flakes (optional)

1. Freeze the steak for half an hour to make it easier to slice, then cut against the grain into ⅛-inch-thick strips. (Or have the butcher cut it at the meat counter.) Put the steak strips in a large zip-top plastic bag.

2. In a small bowl, whisk the soy sauce together with the remaining ingredients. Pour into the zip-top bag with the meat strips and squeeze out the air, making make sure the meat is covered evenly. Refrigerate overnight.

3. If you want to use a dehydrator, arrange the steak in a single layer on the trays, then dehydrate according to the manufacturer's instructions (it should be around 8 hours at 165°F). The jerky is done when it is firm and dry but still slightly pliable.

4. If you prefer to use the oven, preheat to 175°F with the racks in the lower-middle and upper-middle positions. Line a pair of baking sheets with foil and set a wire rack on each. Arrange the steak strips in a single layer on the racks. Cook for 4 hours, or until the meat is firm and dry but still slightly pliable, flipping the pieces over halfway through the cooking time.

5. Transfer the finished jerky to a sealed container and store in the refrigerator. Use within 4 weeks.

BEET THIS

BEET FRIES

It's a real shame that potatoes are superior to beets for frying—potatoes achieve an unbeatable crisp that the Schrutes have spent over two milliennia trying to match, unsuccessfully. But since beets are still better than potatoes in every other category, we endorse these slightly soggy but nutritious beet fries.

Serves 4 ⫿ Prep time: 10 minutes ⫿ Cook time: 30 to 40 minutes

1 pound red beets

⅔ pound golden beets

½ cup olive oil

1 tablespoon sea salt

½ teaspoon black pepper

1. Preheat the oven to 450°F.

2. Cut the beets into ⅛-inch strips. Place in a large mixing bowl along with the olive oil, sea salt, and pepper. Stir to coat evenly.

3. Spread the beets onto a baking sheet lined with 1 sheet of parchment paper, making sure they don't touch each other. Bake 30 to 40 minutes, flipping occasionally to prevent burning and to make sure browning occurs on all sides.

4. Serve your fries along with whatever dipping sauce you choose.

BEET CHIPS

Looking to spice up a festive event such as a calf branding, a deed signing, or a funeral? Look no further than this recipe for a crispy, nutritious alternative to regular potato chips. Oven-baked beet chips can be enjoyed alone or paired with your favorite creamy dipping sauce as a gourmet appetizer. All you need to make these crunchy chips are beets, oil, and salt.

Serves 4 ⧗ Prep time: 20 minutes, plus 20 minutes to marinate ⧗ Cook time: 50 minutes

6 medium beets   2 teaspoons salt

½ cup olive oil

1. Line 2 baking sheets with parchment paper. Cut off the beet tops and scrub the beets using a vegetable brush.

2. Cut the beets as thin as you can, using a mandoline slicer (1/16 inch is best). You don't need to peel the beets for slices this thin. If you don't have a mandoline, use your sharpest knife—and watch your fingers!

3. Place the sliced beets in a medium bowl and add the oil and salt. Toss well and let marinate for 20 minutes. Preheat your oven to 300°F.

4. Toss the beets once more and then pour off the liquid. Arrange the slices in a single layer on the parchment-lined baking sheets.

5. Bake for 25 minutes, then flip them over. Bake for another 25 minutes, or until the chips are crisp but not browned. Let cool completely before serving. Store leftovers in an airtight container.

BEET GREEN CHIPS

Did you make a batch of beet chips and throw away the greens? Idiot. Go to your compost pile and dig them out for another crispy treat. These paper-thin chips melt in your mouth the same way they would slowly decompose in the garden—effortlessly. Sprinkle on your favorite seasonings, such as curry powder, Parmesan cheese, or lime zest and cayenne pepper, right before baking.

Serves 4 | Prep time: 10 minutes | Cook time: 5 to 10 minutes

1 bunch beet greens

nonstick baking spray

sea salt (or smoked sea salt), to taste

black pepper, to taste

1. Preheat the oven to 350°F and line a baking sheet with parchment paper.

2. Wash the beet greens and dry well with paper towels. Remove and discard the stems.

3. Arrange the greens on the prepared baking sheet in a single layer and spray lightly with nonstick baking spray. Sprinkle on a pinch of salt and pepper and your preferred seasonings, then bake for 5 minutes. Check the greens and give them a few more minutes if needed. Keep an eye on them, because these chips can burn fast.

4. Flip them over and bake for another couple of minutes, or until crisp. Let the beet green chips cool down before serving. They will stay crunchy for several hours, then gradually lose their crispiness.

BEET THIS

KARTOFFELPUFFER (GERMAN POTATO PANCAKES)

A favorite Honesdale street food, these potato pancakes are made with finely grated potatoes, eggs, onion, and flour—an ideal nutritional pick-me-up. Enjoy them hot, sweetened with applesauce, or as an accompaniment to meat and gravy, or cold, as a quick pocket snack out in the unforgiving bush.

Serves 4 | Prep time: 15 minutes | Cook time: 8 minutes

2½ pounds russet potatoes

1 medium yellow onion, finely minced

2 large eggs

¼ cup all-purpose flour, or more as needed

1 teaspoon salt

oil, for frying

1. Peel and finely grate the raw potatoes. Place in a colander and squeeze out the excess liquid, using your hands. Or you can wrap them in a clean tea towel to squeeze out the liquid. Squeeze hard—there is more liquid than you might expect!

2. Transfer the potatoes to a large bowl and add the minced onion, eggs, flour, and salt. Combine well, using your hands. You can add more flour if the mixture seems excessively sticky.

3. Heat 3 tablespoons of oil in a nonstick skillet over moderate to high heat.

4. Scoop ½ cup of the potato mixture into the pan for each pancake and use the back of a spoon to flatten it. Fry for about 4 minutes per side, or until golden, and transfer to paper towels to drain. Repeat with the remaining potato mixture, adding more oil if needed. Serve hot.

BUTTERBREZEL

Bavarian pretzels are exactly like wood lice—crispy on the outside and soft and delicious on the inside. Whether you make them for Oktoberfest or harvest Festspiele, this classic dish is always a hit. These are good served German-style, dipped in mustard or melted cheddar cheese and paired with a mug of beet beer.

Serves 6 ❦ Prep time: 35 minutes ❦ Cook time: 8 to 10 minutes

3 cups all-purpose flour, divided, or more as needed

1 teaspoon sugar

1 tablespoon active dry yeast

4 tablespoons (2 ounces) softened butter, divided

4⅓ cups water, divided

1 tablespoon plus ¼ teaspoon coarse salt, divided

3 tablespoons baking soda

1. In a medium bowl, mix 1 cup of flour with the sugar, yeast, and 2 tablespoons of butter. Mix in 1⅓ cups of water and then let the mixture sit for 15 minutes, or until you start to see bubbles.

2. Stir in ¼ teaspoon of salt and then add the remaining flour, bit by bit, until the dough develops a kneadable texture. Knead it on a floured countertop or other surface until elastic, about 8 minutes, adding more flour if necessary.

3. Divide the dough into 6 equal pieces and let rest for 5 minutes. Roll 1 piece of dough into a 15-inch-long rope, then loop and twist it into a pretzel shape. Repeat with the remaining pieces.

4. Preheat the oven to 450°F. Grease your baking sheet.

5. Meanwhile, bring the remaining 3 cups of water to a boil on the stovetop. Sprinkle in the baking soda and stir; remove from the heat. Dip each pretzel into this warm water bath for about 45 seconds, flipping over halfway through to evenly cover.

6. Arrange the pretzels on the baking sheet. Melt the remaining 2 tablespoons of butter and brush onto both sides of the pretzels. Sprinkle with 1 tablespoon of salt and bake for 8 to 10 minutes, or until golden brown.

BEET BREAD

We know what you're thinking—beet bread? What is this, communist Sweden? The truth is, beet bread has been made for centuries by communists and freemen alike. These flaky red loaves are packed with apple juice, pear, walnuts, lemon, and ginger and are perfect for breakfast, lunch, second lunch, afternoon snack, dinner, or second dinner. For a real treat, try spreading some freshly churned, tangy goat butter on a toasted slice of beet bread.

Makes 1 loaf 〰 Prep time: 30 minutes 〰
Cook time: 1 hour, 45 minutes

2 small beets	⅓ cup apple juice
1 small pear, peeled and cored	9½ ounces (2⅛ cups) all-purpose flour

BEET THIS

¼ teaspoon baking soda	2½ ounces chopped walnuts
2 teaspoons baking powder	¼ cup sugar
zest of 1½ lemons, grated	2 eggs
⅓ teaspoon salt	⅓ cup olive oil
2 teaspoons ground ginger	

1. Preheat the oven to 425°F. Grease a 9-inch loaf pan and line it with parchment paper.

2. Roast the beets on a baking sheet for 45 minutes, or until tender. Turn the oven temperature down to 350°F. Remove the beets from the oven and let cool, then peel and transfer to a food processor along with the pear and the apple juice. Purée until smooth.

3. In a large bowl, whisk together the flour, baking soda, baking powder, lemon zest, salt, ginger, and walnuts. Add the sugar, eggs, olive oil, and beet mixture, stirring for a couple of minutes or until the dry ingredients are just mixed in. The batter should be lumpy. Don't overmix, or the bread will be too dense.

4. Transfer the batter into the prepared loaf pan and use the back of a spoon to level out the top. Bake for 1 hour in the center of the oven. Let the beet bread cool for 10 minutes in the pan, then remove from the pan and transfer to a cooling rack. Don't slice until the bread is completely cool.

ROMAN BEETS WITH RAISIN WINE FROTH

The Romans introduced the world to a lot of extraordinary things, such as gladiators, courier services, and durable concrete. Not to mention plumbing, surgical instruments, and the inspiration for season 4, episode 4 of *Battlestar Galactica*. This dish, Roman Beets with Raisin Wine Froth, is not one of the Romans' great inventions. But it is edible.

Serves 4 ▮ Prep time: 5 minutes ▮ Cook time: 35 to 40 minutes

2 tablespoons olive oil

1 medium yellow onion, thinly sliced

2½ pounds beets, peeled and cut into 1-inch pieces

1 cup vegetable broth

1¼ cups sweet raisin wine

1 bay leaf

1 tablespoon sugar

2 fresh thyme sprigs

½ teaspoon black peppercorns

1. Heat the oil in a heavy skillet pan over medium to high heat. Add the onion and cook for 5 minutes, stirring occasionally.

2. Add the beets to the pan along with all the remaining ingredients. Bring the mixture to a boil, then turn the heat down, cover the pan, and simmer for 30 minutes or until the beets are tender.

3. Lift the cooked beets from the pan into a medium serving dish. Turn the temperature under the pan up to high and boil the remaining liquid until it has been reduced by half. Pour the sauce over the beets and stir, making sure to fully coat them, and serve warm.

SWEET AND SOUR BEETS

Fact: The human mouth can only detect five flavors—sweet, salty, sour, bitter, and umami. FALSE. The human mouth can actually detect at least *nine* flavors, including sweet, salty, sour, bitter, umami, deception, fear, adrenaline, and blood. If crafted correctly, this deceptively simple dish balances all of those flavors.

Serves 4 | Prep time: 5 minutes | Cook time: 35 to 45 minutes

3 medium whole beets, tops removed

¼ cup beet cooking water

⅓ cup sugar

½ teaspoon salt

1 tablespoon cornstarch

¼ cup dry white wine

2 teaspoons grated orange zest

1 tablespoon butter

black pepper, to taste

1. Boil the whole beets in a medium pot of water for 30 minutes, or until tender. Remove from the water to cool, saving ¼ cup of the cooking water. Peel the cooled beets, then slice or chop them.

2. In a medium bowl, combine the sugar with the salt and cornstarch. Stir in enough of the wine to make a smooth paste. Gradually whisk in the remaining wine and the reserved cooking water.

3. Pour the mixture into a medium saucepan and simmer gently, stirring often, for 5 minutes or until the liquid is clear. (Pour in more water if the liquid evaporates.) Now stir in the beets, orange zest, and butter. Cook until the beets are warmed through. Season with pepper.

BEET PICKLES

Schrutes are renowned for telling jokes. It's one of our favorite pastimes. Here's one: Did you hear about the guy who stopped eating vegetables? His heart missed a beet. That guy was *Onkel* Schrute, a celebrated carnivore who succumbed to heart disease at the age of 26. Pickled beets are good for your daily health and a critical addition to any properly stocked survival pantry.

Feel free to mix up the spices. Instead of sugar and salt, try onion and garlic. They all make for a delicious brine.

Makes 1 jar ⸮ Prep time: 5 minutes ⸮ Cook time: 5 minutes

½ cup white vinegar

½ cup water

¼ cup sugar

¼ teaspoon salt

1 stick cinnamon

1 teaspoon whole all-spice

6 whole cloves

1 pound small beets, boiled, peeled, and thinly sliced

1. In a small saucepan, bring the vinegar, ½ cup water, sugar, salt, and spices to a boil. Simmer for 5 minutes.

2. Fill sterilized jars with the beet slices and hot liquid, leaving room at the top. Seal. Store in the refrigerator for up to 6 weeks.

BUTTERED BEETS

Buttered Beets is far more than a dish containing butter and beets. It contains butter. And beets. And they are combined. Together.

Serves 5 ⦙ Prep time: 5 minutes ⦙ Cook time: 5 minutes

2 pounds beets, boiled, peeled, and sliced

2 tablespoons (1 ounce) butter

salt, to taste

black pepper, to taste

1. In a medium saucepan, melt the butter over medium-high heat.

2. Add the beets and warm for 5 minutes, turning to coat with the butter. Season with salt and pepper to serve.

BEET THIS

CRIMSON CREAMED BEETS

Some people call these "Harvard Beets" because they are crimson-colored, which is Harvard's official color. You know what we say to those people? Shut. Up. The Schrute Family's official coat of arms—which has been around since at least the early medieval era, when we were all knights—is awash in crimson. You know when Harvard adopted the color crimson? It was in 1910, at least 700 years after the Schrute Family did so.

Serves 4 | Prep time: 5 minutes | Cook time: 14 minutes

2 tablespoons (1 ounce) butter

1 medium yellow onion, finely chopped

2 tablespoons all-purpose flour

1¼ cups whole milk

2 tablespoons heavy cream

salt and black pepper, to taste

1 teaspoon mixed dried herbs

1 pound beets, boiled, peeled, and diced

1 apple, peeled and diced

1. Melt the butter in a small pan, then add the chopped onion and sauté for 5 minutes without letting it brown. Now stir in the flour and cook for 2 minutes, stirring constantly.

2. Remove the pan from the heat and gradually pour in the milk, stirring well. Return the pan to the heat and bring the mixture to a boil, stirring all the while. Turn the heat down and simmer for 2 minutes. Stir in the cream, salt, pepper, and herbs. Add the beets and apple and simmer for another 5 minutes until thickened. Serve hot or warm.

POLISH ĆWIKŁA

What is the best Polish invention? The paperclip, obviously. (The exact origins of the paperclip are disputed, but the International Pulp & Paper Association credits Polish composer Józef Hofmann.) What is the second best Polish invention? Ćwikła. Pronounced CHEEK-wah, Ćwikła is a sweet-and-spicy relish made of beets and horseradish root—two of the more superior roots. Try Polish Ćwikła as a spread on your favorite sandwich or as a topping on everyday beef dishes such as tongue, shank, or shin.

Makes 2 small jars 🥄 Prep time: 5 minutes

1 teaspoon brown sugar

2 cups grated horseradish

1 teaspoon white vinegar

¼ teaspoon salt

1 pound beets, boiled, peeled, and grated

1. Combine the brown sugar, horseradish, vinegar, and salt in a small bowl. Stir in the grated beets.

2. Use within 2 weeks. Serve the Ćwikła cold or warm, as a condiment for a Horsemeat Burger (page 92).

SAUTÉED BEET GREENS

Noted survey voyageur Charles Darwin once said, "A man who dares waste 1 hour of time has not discovered the value of life." That is a misappropriation of a famous Schrute quote: "A man who dares waste one edible portion of the beetroot is an idiot." Don't be an idiot. Eat your beet greens.

Serves 2 | Prep time: 10 minutes | Cook time: 8 to 11 minutes

1 bunch (about 2 cups) fresh beet greens

1 tablespoon olive oil

⅛ teaspoon dried red pepper flakes

2 cloves garlic, minced

salt, to taste

finely grated lemon zest (optional)

1. Wash the beet greens well to remove any dirt or grit, then strip the thicker stems away from the leaves and discard any tough parts. Dice the remaining stems finely and set to one side. Roughly chop the tender leaves.

2. Heat the oil in a medium skillet over low to moderate heat. Stir in the red pepper flakes and garlic. Sauté for 20 seconds or so, stirring all the while. Stir in the diced stems and cook for 3 minutes.

3. Now add the chopped tender leaves along with a pinch of salt, using tongs to toss and coat the leaves in the oil. Cook until the greens are tender and wilted, about 5 to 8 minutes. Taste; add more salt if needed. Serve, garnished with a little lemon zest if desired.

WHOLE ROASTED BEETS

If this recipe were a bear, it would be a black bear. Yes, there are fiercer bears, such as the brown bear; larger bears, such as the grizzly; and cooler bears, such as the sloth bear. But the black bear has better eyesight than humans, is an excellent fisher, and has killed and eaten a jaguar. This dish is exactly like the black bear: unremarkable at first sight but totally badass upon further examination. Save your best and biggest beets for this deceptively simple showstopper.

Serves 6 ǁ Prep time: 5 minutes ǁ
Cook time: 1 hour to 1 hour, 30 minutes

6 large beets, peeled and trimmed

½ cup olive oil

salt and black pepper, to taste

1. Preheat the oven to 400°F.

2. In a large bowl, toss the beets with olive oil. Sprinkle with salt and pepper, then wrap each beet in aluminum foil.

3. Roast the beets for 1 to 1½ hours depending on their size, or until tender. Serve hot.

PICKLED MANGELWURZEL

Have you ever wondered why your farm animals are under-producing milk? Well, it's most likely because you're not feeding them young mangelwurzel, a farmland beet varietal that maximizes milk production in barnyard and farmland ungulates.

But the magic of mangelwurzel doesn't stop with animals. Humans can eat it, too—especially if you pluck the mangel-wurzel when it's young! In fact, just as it does for domesticated animals, mangelwurzel maximizes milk production in *human* females, too. In the Schrute family, we have a saying: "Maximize your milk, maximize the size and strength of your offspring!"

Serves 4 ⫙ Prep time: 10 minutes ⫙ Cook time: 5 minutes

1 mangelwurzel	1 teaspoon salt
½ cup white wine vinegar	⅛ teaspoon black pepper
½ cup water	1 tablespoon sugar

1. Wash the mangelwurzel and put it in a small saucepan. Pour in enough water to cover by 1 inch and cook over medium-high until tender. Remove the mangelwurzel from the pan; when it is cool enough to handle, peel and slice. Rinse out the pan.

2. Combine the vinegar, water, salt, pepper, and sugar in the same pan and bring to a boil. Pour the mixture over the mangelwurzel slices and let cool completely.

BEET THIS

3. This will keep for several weeks stored in the refrigerator in a clean glass jar with a tight-fitting lid. You can serve the pickled mangelwurzel cold or warm it up.

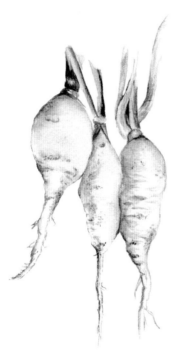

FIRE ROASTED BEETS

Fire roasted beets are a delicious alternative to boiled beets. But this recipe also offers a superior opportunity for a Fire Safety Teaching Moment! While the beets are cooking, light a small, contained fire in your garbage can. Now see who in your household can properly and efficiently extinguish the flames. This is a great way to find out which of your kitchen subordinates were paying attention during your kitchen safety talk.*

Serves 4 ⏐ Prep time: 10 minutes ⏐ Cook time: 1 hour

4 large beets, halved lengthwise

salt and black pepper, to taste

1 tablespoon olive oil

1. Preheat the oven to 375°F. Place the beets in a bowl and toss with the oil and some salt and pepper.

2. Top a large piece of aluminum foil with a sheet of parchment paper. Wrap the foil around the beets and seal. Roast for 1 hour, or until the beets are cooked through. Unwrap the beets and rub them with paper towels—the skin should peel right off.

3. Serve these beets warm as a side dish with meat or fish, or chill and add them to a salad.

*Publisher's Disclaimer: Opinions and suggestions stated here are the authors' alone, do not reflect those of the publisher, and should not be taken seriously.

BEET THIS

SOUPS
AND STEWS

FACT: Seventy-five percent of Americans are chronically dehydrated. Mild dehydration can cause irritability, constipation, lethargy, mental fog, and diminished reflexes. Combined, these often lead to death at the hands of a more hydrated villain. This chapter turns the tables with a simple but genius plan—adding water to food in the form of hearty, nutritious soups and stews. Read on. One day, soup may literally save your life.

BORSCHT

You can't talk about borscht without talking about the Ukraine. And, of course, you can't talk about the Ukraine without mentioning that country's biggest addition to the superhero canon—the invention of the X-ray by Ivan Puluj, allowing mortals to see inside the human body, mind, and soul. But before the X-ray, Ukrainians invented the soup called borscht. Was borscht the inspiration for the X-ray? We may never know. What we do know is that borscht was originally made with the stems and umbels of common hogweed. Today it is made with beetroot, beef, and sautéed vegetables. A slight improvement.

Serves 8 ｜ Prep time: 25 minutes ｜ Cook time: 1 hour, 25 minutes

1 pound ground pork sausage

3 large beets, peeled and shredded

3 medium russet potatoes, peeled and cubed

BEET THIS

3 carrots, peeled and shredded

½ head cabbage, cored and shredded

1 (14.5-ounce) can diced tomatoes, drained

1 tablespoon olive oil

1 large yellow onion, chopped

¾ cup water

1 (6-ounce) can tomato paste

3 cloves garlic, minced

1 teaspoon sugar, or as needed

salt and black pepper, to taste

½ cup sour cream, for serving

1 tablespoon chopped fresh parsley, for garnish

1. Crumble the sausage into a small pan over moderately high heat and cook, stirring until browned. Remove from heat and set to one side.

2. Fill a large cooking pot halfway with water and bring to a boil. Add the sausage, cover the pot, and bring back to a boil. Next add the beets, cover, and simmer for about 1 hour. Add the potatoes and carrots, cover, and cook for 15 minutes. Stir in the cabbage and the drained tomatoes.

3. Heat the olive oil in a small skillet over moderate heat, then add the chopped onion and sauté until tender. Stir in the ¾ cup water and the tomato paste, then transfer the mixture to the large pot. Add the raw minced garlic, cover the pot, and turn off the heat.

4. Let the borscht stand for 5 minutes, then uncover and add sugar, salt, and pepper to taste. Serve in bowls, garnished with sour cream and parsley.

RUSSIAN BEET SOUP

It's rumored that this recipe was brought back to the farm from a ski vacation to a gulag in Eastern Siberia. There's no better nourishment after a long, cold day of mogul runs or forced manual labor. A real time-tested winner.

Serves 4 ⎪ Prep time: 5 minutes ⎪ Cook time: 20 to 30 minutes

8 cups chicken broth

5 medium beets, boiled, peeled, and sliced

juice of 1 lemon

ground cinnamon, to taste

ground nutmeg, to taste

1 cup dry red wine

1 teaspoon brown sugar

1. In a small pot, heat the chicken broth over medium-high heat. Add the chopped beets along with the lemon juice and some cinnamon and nutmeg. Return the broth to a boil for 15 minutes

2. Add a cup of red wine, sweetened with a teaspoonful of brown sugar. Let simmer for 2 to 5 minutes and serve while hot.

BEET AND BEEF STEW

At first glance, this stew might seem similar to borscht (page 58). After all, both contain beets and meat, and both are stews. So what? Would you say that a wolverine is similar to a bear? Of course you wouldn't. You know that wolverines are of the Mustelidae family, whereas bears are of the Ursidae family. A child wouldn't make that mistake. Speaking of bears and wolverines, both are excellent replacements for the beef in this dish.

Serves 4 ⎸ Prep time: 10 minutes ⎸ Cook time: 3 hours, 40 minutes

2 pounds beef stew meat

salt and black pepper, to taste

1 teaspoon ground ginger

1½ teaspoons caraway seeds

¼ teaspoon ground cinnamon

3 tablespoons olive oil

2 tablespoons sugar

2 small sweet onions, diced

2 tablespoons red wine vinegar

1 tablespoon minced garlic

5 cups cold water

3 white potatoes, peeled and diced

2 carrots, peeled and diced

2 medium beets, peeled and diced

fresh chopped parsley and dill, for serving (optional)

1. Sprinkle salt, pepper, ginger, caraway seeds, and cinnamon on both sides of the beef. Heat a large pot over moderate heat and then add the olive oil. Add the meat, turning to brown on both sides.

2. Next add the sugar, onions, vinegar, garlic, and water. Bring to a simmer and skim off any foam. Cover and simmer gently over low heat for 3 hours, stirring occasionally.

3. Add the diced potatoes, carrots, and beets to the pot. Taste and add more salt, pepper, and/or spices if needed. Lift the meat out of the pot and onto a cutting board to break it into smaller pieces, then mix it back into the stew and cook for another 30 minutes.

4. Serve in warmed bowls, garnished with parsley and dill if you wish.

PFEFFERPOTTHAST

When your guests eat this dish, they will undoubtedly say something to the effect of "Wow, that is so incredible! That's amazing! The stew is so thick! What's your secret?" You will not tell them. Instead, you will offer them a wry smile, knowing that the secret to this rich, flavorful stew is that it is uniquely thickened with pumpernickel crumbs, not something as basic as regular old flour or sourdough.

Serves 8   Prep time: 10 minutes   Cook time: 1 hour, 20 minutes

4 large onions

3 pounds beef stew meat, cut in 1-inch cubes

¾ teaspoon ground allspice, or more as needed

2 bay leaves

juice of 1 lemon, or more as needed

2 teaspoons salt, or more as needed

1 tablespoon black pepper, or more as needed

1½ cups beef stock, or more as needed

1½ cups dry white wine, or more as needed

2 or 3 tablespoons pumpernickel breadcrumbs, fresh

1 tablespoon sugar (optional)

1. Finely chop 2 of the onions and thinly slice the other 2. Add the beef cubes to a large pot along with the onions, allspice, bay leaves, lemon juice, salt, and pepper.

2. Pour in the beef stock and wine; it should just cover the beef cubes. Stir to mix well. Cook for 1 hour over low to medium heat, covered, and stir occasionally. If there's not enough liquid in the pan to make a sauce, you can add more stock, wine, or water during cooking.

3. Remove the bay leaves. Stir in the breadcrumbs and cook for 20 minutes longer to let the sauce thicken. Taste and add more salt, pepper, lemon juice, and/or allspice if needed. Add the sugar, too, if you like. Ladle into bowls to serve.

PENNSYLVANIA POT PIE

How many crusts do you think this pot pie has—one? Wrong. The answer is zero, idiot. Here in Dutch Pennsylvania, we sneak the crust *inside* the pot pie in the form of the clandestine dough noodle. Aside from being the slyest of pot pies, the Pennsylvania pot pie offers a great use for leftover scraps of meat, potatoes, and various vegetables. This recipe calls for ham, but other meats are also acceptable.

Serves 4 to 6 ⏐ Prep time: 15 minutes ⏐ Cook time: 15 minutes

1 pound cooked ham

4 medium russet potatoes, peeled and diced into chunks

1 medium onion, finely chopped

3 cups vegetable stock, or more as needed

2 cups all-purpose flour

½ teaspoon salt, plus more to taste

3 eggs, lightly beaten

¼ cup water

1 tablespoon finely chopped fresh parsley

black pepper, to taste

1. Place a large saucepan over medium heat and add the ham, potatoes, onion, and vegetable stock. Bring to a simmer and cook until the potatoes are nearly tender, about 10 minutes.

2. In a medium mixing bowl, combine the flour with ½ teaspoon of salt. Create a well in the center and add the eggs and water. Gradually bring the mixture together to form a dough. Turn out onto a work surface and roll to ⅛-inch thickness, then use a knife to slice the dough into small, approximately 2-inch squares.

3. Turn up the heat on the saucepan and bring to a rapid boil. Transfer the homemade noodle squares into the saucepan one at a time. Reduce the heat to a low simmer for 5 minutes, adding extra stock if needed to keep it slowly boiling. (Note: The dough will make the liquid thicker.) Season the potpie with parsley, salt, and pepper, and serve.

MAINS

A great Schrute once said that there are eight basic biological needs for human survival: air, water, shelter, sex, clothing, survival skills, and meat. You may have noticed that there are only *seven* items on that list. Very good. Originally sleep was included, but that was later scrapped when Dwide Schrute proved beyond a reasonable doubt that sleep was, in fact, in no way necessary to survival. This chapter satisfies all your needs. Enjoy.

RUSSIAN STUFFED TONGUE

It is a well-known fact that fresh beef tongue was the meal of choice for most of the motherland's most successful dictators. When eaten immediately before an important speech, beef tongue is proven to grant you powers of persuasion and enhanced eloquence. If you're not a dictator but just a boring, normal person, enjoy this dish before a Zoom meeting, or something.

Serves 8 ❧ Prep time: 1 hour, 20 minutes ❧
Cook time: 2 hours, 30 minutes to 4 hours, 30 minutes

1 raw beef tongue (about 2 pounds)

1 large yellow onion, chopped

2 cloves garlic, chopped

1 cup fresh breadcrumbs

1 egg

4 tablespoons (2 ounces) butter, divided

2 tablespoons fresh sage, chopped

2 tablespoons fresh thyme, chopped

salt and black pepper, to taste

10 whole cloves

2 tablespoons white vinegar

sliced boiled beets, pitted olives, and/or fresh parsley, for garnish (optional)

1. Soak the tongue in a large bowl of cold water for 1 hour. Use a knife to scrape it clean, then rinse under cold running water.

2. To make the stuffing, add the onion, garlic, breadcrumbs, egg, 2 tablespoons of butter, sage, thyme, and the salt and pepper to the bowl of a food processor. Pulse a few times until roughly mixed. Cut a slit in the tongue lengthwise and fill with the stuffing mixture. Stitch closed with cooking twine, or use toothpicks or metal skewers to hold it closed.

3. Bring a large pot of water to a simmer, add the tongue, and cook for 15 minutes. Drain the pot, refill with new water, and simmer the tongue gently for 2 to 4 hours or until tender, checking occasionally and adding water if needed. To check whether the tongue is done, pierce the thickest part with a knife. If the juices are not clear, it is not yet done.

4. When the tongue is nearly tender, remove the skin. It should come off easily when the tongue is almost done. Firmly stick the cloves all over the tongue and simmer for another 15 minutes.

5. Melt the remaining 2 tablespoons of butter in a small pan and combine it with the vinegar. Remove the tongue from the cooking water and drain well, then rub the vinegar-butter mixture over the surface. Cut the tongue into slices and serve warm, garnished with sliced beets, pitted olives, and/or parsley sprigs, if desired.

STUFFED BEETS

Is this recipe a Schrute original? No, it was invented by the French. However, it was *stolen* from the French by Schrute legend Brock Larsen Schrute in 1781, during what can only be described as the perfect crime. In short, Brock infiltrated the Louvre, made love to Marie Antoinette, and stole a recipe book from King Louis's head chef. Iconic.

Serves 4 ⧚ Prep time: 15 minutes ⧚

8 medium beets, boiled and peeled

1 teaspoon salt

2 cups red wine vinegar

1 shallot, finely chopped

1 cucumber, peeled and finely chopped

¼ cup finely chopped fresh dill, plus more for garnish

1 head iceberg lettuce, broken into leaves

BEET THIS

FRENCH DRESSING

1 tablespoon white wine vinegar

1 teaspoon Dijon mustard

½ teaspoon smoked paprika

¼ teaspoon salt

3 tablespoons olive oil

1. Place the beets in a medium container. Cover with salt and red wine vinegar and allow the beets to cool completely. The longer the beets sit in the red wine vinegar, the stronger the pickled flavor will be.

2. As the beets cool, prepare the dressing. In a small jug, whisk together the white wine vinegar, mustard, paprika, and salt. Gradually pour in the olive oil, whisking continuously. Taste and adjust the seasoning if needed, then set aside.

3. Use a teaspoon to remove the center of each beet, forming a cup. Take the scooped-out beet portions and use a small star or circular cookie cutter to stamp out shapes; set aside.

4. In a small mixing bowl, stir together the shallot, cucumber, ¼ cup of dill, and French dressing. Fill each beet cup with this mixture, then cover with the stamped-out beet shapes and decorate with additional chopped dill.

5. Arrange a bed of lettuce leaves on a serving plate and top with the stuffed beets.

Cook's Note: The cucumber can be replaced with chopped radish, olives, or celery.

COLD POACHED FISH

The reason this dish is so bad … is BECAUSE IT ISN'T! In fact, it is one of the best uses of leftover fish ever invented. You can use salmon, trout, pike, largemouth bass, muskellunge, hybrid striped bass, non-hybrid striped bass, panfish, walleye, perch, channel catfish, mermaid tail, or even German *karpfen* or *fellchen*.

Serves 8 | Prep time: 30 minutes | Cook time: 18 to 20 minutes

1 small onion, roughly chopped

1 celery stalk, roughly chopped

2 bay leaves

1 teaspoon black peppercorns

1 teaspoon salt

½ cup white wine vinegar

1 whole salmon, approximately 4 pounds,

cleaned and scaled, and gutted

2 cucumbers, thinly sliced

2 cups watercress, whole

1 lemon, cut into wedges

mayonnaise or hollandaise sauce, for serving

sliced boiled beets and lettuce leaves, for serving (optional)

1. In a small saucepan, combine the onion, celery, bay leaves, peppercorns, salt, vinegar, and 3 inches of water. Place over high heat and bring to a boil, then reduce heat and simmer for 10 minutes.

2. Set a fish kettle/poacher or a roasting pan on the stovetop over low heat and add the whole salmon. Cook for 8 to 10 minutes. Pour the hot stock over the fish and cover the kettle with the lid or aluminum foil. Turn the heat off and allow the fish to cool in the stock. Once the stock has cooled, transfer the fish onto a serving platter. Using a spoon, carefully scrape the skin away to expose the delicately cooked flesh.

3. To serve, cover the fish with cucumber slices and create a surrounding bed of watercress; garnish with lemon wedges. Present the whole cold poached fish in the center of the table, along with mayonnaise or hollandaise sauce for serving.

Cook's Note: Salmon can easily be swapped out for trout, pike, or any leftover fish.

Alternate Serving Suggestion: You can scrape the meat from the fish, discarding the bones. Serve on individual plates on a bed of sliced boiled beets and lettuce leaves.

MAINS

PIGEONS IN JELLY

The Schrutes have kept domesticated pigeons on their farmlands and homesteads for well over 10,000 years, breeding them for a range of purposes—exhibitions, sport, meat, and of course, clandestine warfare. This dish, popularized in the early 1900s, allows you to present your most prized pigeons encased in gelatin as a table centerpiece and savory cold starter.

Serves 8 ⫯ Prep time: 6 hours, 30 minutes ⫯
Cook time: 4 hours, 30 minutes

4 whole pigeons (about 1 pound each), legs and wings tied

2 bay leaves, divided

1 bunch fresh thyme, divided

pinch of salt

8 ounces of veal bones

1 calf's foot

2 carrots, roughly chopped

2 medium onions, roughly chopped

2 celery stalks, roughly chopped

1 teaspoon black peppercorns

½ teaspoon whole cloves

1 bunch fresh parsley, divided

1 gallon water, or as needed

crackers or toast, for serving

1. Place the whole pigeons, bay leaf, and half of the thyme in a large saucepan. Cover with cold water and add a pinch of salt. Turn the heat under the pan to high and bring the water to a boil. Skim off any scum that rises to the top and then turn the heat to low so that the water is gently simmering. Poach the pigeons for 30 minutes, until fully cooked or the pigeon reaches an internal temperature of 165°F when measured with a meat thermometer.

2. Remove the pigeons from the pan and allow to rest for 10 minutes. Then carve, keeping the meat in large pieces if

BEET THIS

possible. Remove all the meat from the bones and set aside; discard the carcass and skin.

3. Pour the cooking liquid through a sieve into a large saucepan or stockpot; discard the solids left in the sieve. Return the stock to the stovetop over medium-high heat and add the veal bones, calf's foot, carrots, onions, celery, peppercorns, cloves, the remaining thyme, ½ bunch of parsley, bay leaf, and enough water to cover. Bring to a boil, then reduce the heat and simmer for 4 hours, skimming regularly.

4. Strain the stock to remove all the solids, then return the liquid to the stove over medium-high heat. Reduce to 4 cups, remove from the heat, and let cool.

5. Line a terrine mold with plastic wrap and neatly arrange the pigeon meat inside. Add the remaining parsley, finely chopped, and then pour in the veal stock. Place in the refrigerator and chill for at least 6 hours to let the gelatin set.

6. To serve, loosen the jellied pigeons from the mold by lifting the plastic wrap. Invert onto a serving platter and cut into slices. Serve with crackers or toasted bread.

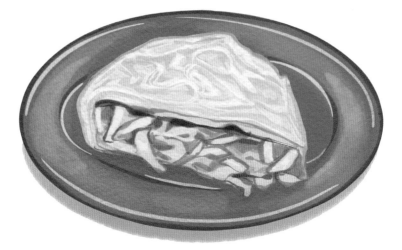

CABBAGE PIE

This dish is cheap, boring, and unremarkable, just like most of your friends. For this reason, it is a great dish to serve to your friends, especially when they come over unannounced. Utilizing onion, cabbage, and almost nothing else of note, cabbage pie is perhaps the least delicious pie ever invented. Serve with lukewarm cow's milk, the least remarkable of the milks.

Serves 8 | Prep time: 15 minutes | Cook time: 1 hour, 15 minutes

3 tablespoons butter

1 small head of green cabbage, finely chopped

3 hard-boiled eggs, peeled and chopped

1 tablespoon chopped fresh dill

salt, to taste

1 teaspoon caraway seeds (optional)

2 sheets frozen yeasted puff pastry

1 egg, beaten

1. Melt the butter in a medium skillet over low to medium heat. Add the cabbage and cook for 30 minutes, stirring occasionally until softened but not browned. Remove the skillet from the heat and let the cabbage cool for 15 minutes.

2. Preheat the oven to 400°F. Mix the hard-boiled eggs and dill into the cabbage and season with salt. Add the caraway seeds as well, if using.

3. Line a pie plate with a sheet of puff pastry. Spoon in the cabbage mixture. Cover with the second sheet of pastry and pinch the edges together. Brush beaten egg over the top. Bake for 45 minutes, or until golden brown.

PHILADELPHIA PEPPER POT

While no Schrute has ever been allowed to set foot in the Quaker City, nor would care to, cousin Reinhold's first wife, Mary, has vouched for this recipe. Her cooking is respectable, so we are including it. This dish will take two days to complete.

Serves 4 ⦙ Prep time: 20 minutes ⦙ Cook time: 12 hours

2 pounds plain beef tripe

2 pounds honeycomb tripe

1 veal knuckle

1 large onion, chopped

1 bay leaf

4 medium white potatoes, peeled and cubed

1 cup chopped fresh parsley

1 cup chopped fresh thyme

1 red bell pepper, halved and seeded

salt, to taste

cayenne pepper, to taste

2 cups all-purpose flour, plus more for rolling the dumplings

½ pound beef suet, finely chopped

DAY 1

1. Place the tripe in a large pot and cover with water. Cover and simmer for 8 hours. Continuously add more water to cover the beef as it begins to evaporate. Remove the tripe to a cutting board and let cool fully before cutting into small squares (about ¾ inch). Refrigerate in a sealed container.

DAY 2

2. Wash the veal knuckle and place it in a large pot. Add enough cold water to cover the knuckle, cover, then bring to a low simmer

BEET THIS

over medium-low heat; continue cooking for 3 hours. Skim the knuckle scum from the top of the water as it simmers.

3. Remove the veal knuckle from the pot, reserving the broth. Pull the meat from the bone and cut into small pieces, approximately ½ inch. Set aside.

4. Strain the broth and return it to the pot. Toss in the chopped onion and bay leaf, cover, and simmer for 1 hour.

5. After an hour, add the potatoes and herbs (the parsley and thyme are essential). Add the bell pepper, tripe, and veal meat; season with salt and cayenne.

6. To make the dumplings, in a mixing bowl combine the flour, beef suet, and a pinch of salt. Add enough water to be able to roll the dough into marble-sized dumplings. Coat the dumplings with flour to prevent them from sticking together.

7. When all the dumplings are ready, toss them into the pot and cook for 2 minutes. Serve immediately.

STEWED SHIN OF BEEF

How would we describe this dish? Three words: Amazing. Mind-blowing. Awesome. Also totally outstanding. Irresistible. And very good. Simmered with vegetables, herbs, and spices, beef shin makes a hearty, warming stew. Serve it over creamy mashed potatoes.

P.S. Shin of beef is the most underrated cut of beef, chock-full of delicious, chewy connective tissue. Yum!

Serves 6 | Prep time: 20 minutes | Cook time: 6 to 8 hours

BEET THIS

2 quarts water

4 pounds beef shin (ask the butcher to cut the bone into a few pieces)

½ small carrot, peeled and sliced

1 medium yellow onion

1 whole clove

1 bay leaf

1 parsley sprig

1⅓ teaspoon salt

½ teaspoon black pepper

1½ tablespoons butter or pan drippings from the beef

1½ tablespoons all-purpose flour

1. In a large pot, bring the water to a boil, then add everything except the butter and flour. Reduce heat, cover, and simmer gently for 6 to 8 hours. (If you prefer, you can use a slow cooker for this.)

2. In a small saucepan over medium-high heat, combine about ¼ of the pot liquid with the butter and flour to make a gravy. (The remaining liquid can be sieved and used for soup.) Keep simmering and whisking until thickened. Remove from heat.

3. Lift the beef shin out of the pot and remove the marrow and meat from the bone onto a platter. Spoon the vegetables and gravy from the pot into the platter with the meat and serve.

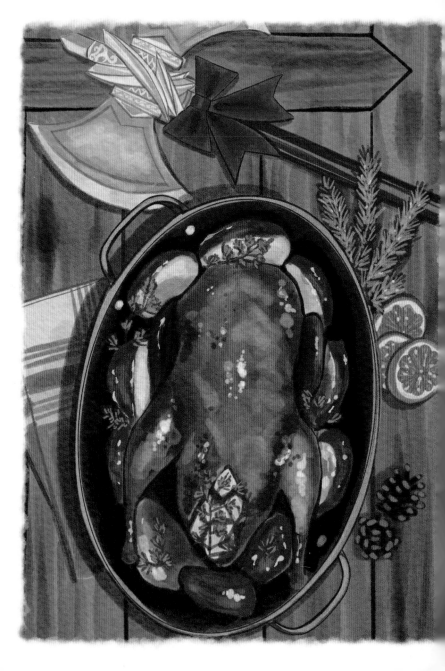

CHRISTMAS GOOSE

America got a lot of things right. A robust justice system, paintball, heavy metal, and *Battlestar Galactica,* to name four. But America got one thing completely wrong. Turkey. To be specific, eating it. On holidays. Turkey should never be eaten. Especially not on festive occasions like Christmas and Ascension Day. Why not? Because turkey is the worst-tasting of all the fowls. Go for this goose instead.

Serves 4 to 6 ▯ Prep time: 1 hour ▯ Cook time: 3 hours

1 goose, about 9 pounds

salt and black pepper, to taste

2 carrots, peeled and cut in half crosswise

2 celery stalks, cut in half crosswise

1 clementine or orange, peeled and quartered

1 whole head garlic, unpeeled and cut in half lengthwise

3 sprigs fresh rosemary

1. Remove the goose from the refrigerator and let it rest on a cutting board for 30 minutes to come to room temperature. Preheat the oven to 400°F.

2. Using a sharp knife, score the skin of the goose in a crisscross pattern, including the underside and legs, without cutting through to the flesh. Remove the neck and tail. Open the body cavity, remove any giblets, and cut away excess fat. Season the cavity with salt and pepper and insert the carrots, celery, clementine or orange, garlic, and rosemary. Using kitchen twine, tie the goose legs together to seal the cavity. Season the outer skin with salt and place the bird on an oven rack set over an oven tray.

3. Roast for 1 hour, until the skin is golden brown. Then reduce the oven temperature to 325°F and cook for an additional 2 hours. (Plan on 20 minutes cooking time per pound.) Baste the pan juices over the goose every 30 minutes, creating a crispy skin and ensuring moist meat. If the goose begins to brown too much, cover lightly with aluminum foil. To check for doneness, use a sharp knife to pierce the thickest part of the thigh; if the juices run clear, the goose is ready. Alternatively, use a thermometer to check the internal temperature of the goose. It should have a minimum of 165°F throughout.

4. Remove the goose from the oven and place on a cutting board. Cover loosely with aluminum foil and let rest for 30 minutes. Then remove the contents of the body cavity; they can be used to create a gravy, if you wish. Present the goose whole as the centerpiece for your Christmas table, to be carved for your guests.

BEET THIS

VEAL LOAF

Known in the Schrute family as "bodybuilder's loaf," this recipe was created in 1742 by Henrietta "The Hammer" Mildred Schrute, who was said to be as strong as an ox and twice as smart. Low in fat and full of protein, this veal loaf is a perfect breakfast for anybody looking to build muscle. For optimal results, eat twice or thrice daily.

Serves 6 ‖ Prep time: 15 minutes ‖ Cook time: 45 minutes

2 pounds ground veal

1½ teaspoons salt

¼ cup lemon juice

¼ cup tomato juice

1 cup dried breadcrumbs

2 eggs

½ cup finely chopped yellow onion

½ cup finely chopped celery

TOMATO SAUCE

2 (28-ounce) cans crushed tomatoes

1 teaspoon dried thyme leaves

1 teaspoon lemon juice

1 small yellow onion, minced

2 cloves garlic, minced

salt and black pepper, to taste

1. Preheat the oven to 350°F.

2. In a large bowl, combine the veal and 1½ teaspoons of salt, using your hands to mix. Then mix in the remaining ingredients, shape into a loaf, and transfer to a 9 x 5-inch, greased loaf pan.

3. In another large bowl, mix the tomato sauce ingredients together. Pour the mixture over the veal loaf. Bake for 45 minutes. Let the loaf cool for at least 15 minutes before slicing and serving.

FRIED PEPPERS WITH PORK CHOPS

Do we think that other pork chop dishes are as good as this one? Well, let's put it this way: no. The recipe calls for four chops, but obviously you should double or triple that depending on how hungry you are. And if you plan to have guests, well, we hope you can do basic mathematics.

Serves 4 ⫙ Prep time: 5 minutes ⫙ Cook time: 21 minutes

4 pork chops, 1½-inches thick

all-purpose flour, as needed

splash of olive oil

4 red bell peppers, seeded and cut in narrow slices

½ to 1 teaspoon minced hot red chili pepper

butter, as needed

1 tablespoon white wine vinegar

salt and freshly ground black pepper, to taste

1. Preheat the oven to 200°F. Dust the pork chops with flour and warm the oil in a medium skillet over medium-high heat. Add the pork chops and cook for 5 minutes per side, or until golden brown. Transfer to a pan, cover, and keep warm in the oven.

2. Add the bell peppers and chili pepper to the same skillet. Sauté over medium-low heat for 10 minutes or until the peppers are tender, stirring often. You can add a little butter if there isn't much oil left in the pan. Stir in the vinegar and grind in some salt and black pepper. Cook for 1 minute longer.

3. Remove the chops from the oven and serve with the pepper mixture spooned on top.

SPICY FRIED RATTLESNAKE WITH PICKLED BEETS

Question: Why are there no venomous snakes in Pennsylvania? TRICK QUESTION. There are three different species of venomous snake in Pennsylvania—timber rattlesnake, Eastern massasauga, and copperhead. They are equally deadly and equally delicious. Timber rattlesnakes are plump and have an exceptionally flavorful meat that pairs well with a mature beet wine.

Serves 6 ▮ Prep time: 5 minutes ▮ Cook time: 8 to 12 minutes

3 pounds rattlesnake, skinned and filleted

oil for frying (canola or peanut oil is best)

1 cup all-purpose flour

1 cup cornmeal

1 teaspoon cayenne pepper

⅛ teaspoon garlic powder

¼ teaspoon ground cumin

⅛ teaspoon sugar

1 teaspoon salt

Beet Pickles (page 47)

1. Pour about 2 inches of oil into a large skillet and heat to approximately 350°F.

2. In a large bowl, mix together the flour, cornmeal, cayenne, garlic powder, cumin, sugar, and salt. Gently toss the snake fillets in this mixture until each piece is evenly coated.

3. Carefully place as many pieces in the pan as will fit without overcrowding. Fry for 8 to 12 minutes, until the snake is a crispy golden brown. Place on paper towels to drain the oil. Serve with pickled beets.

HORSEMEAT BURGER WITH HORSERADISH MUSTARD

Horse burgers are a wonderful on-the-go lunch. One of the leanest meats of any domesticated ungulate, roasted horse breast has just a scintilla of sweetness. It has been compared favorably to the flank of a werewolf that has just eaten a regular wolf. Feel free to dress your burger however you like; but take note that a true horse burger contains only bread, Polish Ćwikła, and meat. Nothing more. Nothing less.

Serves 4 | Prep time: 5 minutes | Cook time: 10 minutes

BEET THIS

1 pound ground horsemeat

½ medium onion, chopped

3 tablespoons chopped fresh parsley

salt and black pepper, to taste

8 slices of bread or 4 hamburger buns

Polish Ćwikła (page 50)

1 tomato, sliced

2 lettuce leaves, shredded

¼ cup crumbled feta cheese

1. In a large bowl, mix the ground meat, onion, and parsley; season with salt and pepper. Mold the mixture into 4 burger patties.

2. Grill for approximately 10 minutes, flipping the patties over halfway through. For optimal taste, the internal temperature of each patty should reach about 160°F. Toast your bread or buns, add the patties, and garnish with ćwikła and your preferred toppings.

PORK KNUCKLE

The best thing about this dish? You can use the leftover pork pieces to make a sandwich, and when some idiot asks what you're eating you can ask them if they'd like to try your knuckle sandwich. Pork knuckle is very tasty, with a crunchy, salty exterior encasing the shockingly juicy meat.

Serves 4 | Prep time: 10 minutes | Cook time: 2 hours, 35 minutes

1 tablespoon caraway seeds

2 juniper berries

2 teaspoons black peppercorns

1 teaspoon salt

2 pork knuckles, about 1½ pounds each

2 small onions, thinly sliced

12-ounce lager (German, if available)

2 bay leaves

1. Preheat the oven to 300°F. Using a pestle and mortar, create the spice mix by grinding together the caraway seeds, juniper berries, peppercorns, and salt. Using a sharp knife, score the skin of the pork knuckles in a crisscross pattern at 1-inch intervals. Rub the spice mix into the skin, making sure it reaches inside the scored gaps.

2. In an ovenproof dish, layer the sliced onions and then top with the pork knuckles, bone facing up. Transfer to the oven, cover, and roast for 1 hour and 30 minutes. Then remove from the oven, pour in the lager, and add the bay leaves. Return to the oven to cook for 1 hour longer.

3. Remove from the oven and transfer the pork knuckles onto a baking tray. Set the oven temperature to broil or to 400°F. Return the pork knuckles to the oven for 5 minutes, until the skin is golden and crispy.

4. To make a gravy (optional), scrape the contents of the dish containing the onions, lager, and pork fat from the knuckles into a blender. Add ½ cup water and blitz until smooth. Serve the beer-and-onion gravy alongside the crispy pork knuckles.

BEET THIS

HOMEMADE BRATWURST FILLING

When a 4-year-old Schrute boy named Banjo ate these sausages for the first time, he ingested them so quickly that his mother, Gertrude, commented that he was "eating pig like a pig." Young Banjo stared at her. "Well, so what, Mother," he snapped. "Pigs are only the smartest even-toed ungulate on the entire planet, so thanks for the compliment! Idiot." This bratwurst recipe includes plenty of herbs and spices to produce a spectacular flavor. The milk powder helps the sausages stay moist, but you can add extra pork fat instead if you prefer.

Makes about 10 (4-inch) links ⚭ Prep time: 1 hour ⚭
Cook time: 15 minutes

2½ pounds boneless pork shoulder, cut in ½-inch chunks

12 ounces pork back fat (fatback), cut in ½-inch chunks

2 cups crushed ice

4 feet of your favorite sausage casing

1½ tablespoons salt

¼ cup dried milk powder

¾ teaspoon mustard powder

¼ teaspoon ground cardamom

¼ teaspoon crushed caraway seeds

1 teaspoon ground mace (or you can use nutmeg as a substitute)

1½ teaspoons white pepper

¾ teaspoon black pepper

1 teaspoon ground ginger

1 teaspoon dried marjoram

¼ teaspoon ground coriander

1. The meat needs to be very cold, so freeze it for 45 minutes before grinding. Then mix the pork shoulder and fatback with the ice in a medium bowl and quickly grind it through a ¼-inch grinding plate (or food processor). It's best to grind into a bowl placed in an ice bath; if the meat isn't very cold, the fat will melt. Grind half of the ground meat again, then mix all together. Refrigerate the meat as soon as it's ground.

2. Mix all the spice mix ingredients together in a small bowl. Now take the meat out of the refrigerator and transfer to the mixing bowl along with spices. Use the mixer's paddle attachment to mix for 3 minutes, or until you see little threads when you pull apart a clump. You can add a little ice water if the meat seems too stiff for mixing. To check the seasoning balance, you can fry a little of

BEET THIS

the ground meat to taste it. Refrigerate the meat while you get the casings ready.

3. Thread the hog casings or whatever type you're using on a sausage stuffer. Then fill the stuffer with the meat and stuff the casings to form 4-inch links.

4. Chill the sausages overnight before cooking them, if you can. Then poach them in slightly salted water or grill or fry them for 15 minutes or until cooked through. We recommend cooking the sausages while the links are still connected. Separate the sausages to serve.

Note: Making extra? You can freeze your bratwursts either before or after cooking them. Then simply thaw overnight in the refrigerator and cook or heat them.

RINDERROULADE

What's better than meat? More meat! This classic Bavarian dish is made by wrapping a slab of beef around German staples such as bacon, onion, mustard, and pickle. Scholars may never learn whether Winston Churchill was referring to the Schrutes or the Russian empire when he said, "It is a riddle wrapped in a mystery inside an enigma." But all agree that he was speaking of this Schrute rinderroulade when he said, "Eating words has never given me indigestion ... but this definitely did." We suggest serving your gravy-topped rinderroulade alongside potatoes, dumplings, or spätzle.

Serves 4 ⦙ Prep time: 30 minutes ⦙ Cook time: 1 hour, 40 minutes

100

BEET THIS

4 thin slices of top round steak, about 4 x 6 inches, pounded to ¼-inch thickness

salt and black pepper, to taste

¼ cup grainy mustard

8 slices bacon

4 German-style pickles, cut into matchstick shapes

1 tablespoon vegetable oil

2 small onions, finely chopped

3 cloves garlic, finely chopped

1 tablespoon tomato paste

1 cup dry red wine

2 cups beef stock

1 bay leaf

4 tablespoons (2 ounces) butter

1. Lay out the round steak slices on a flat surface and season with salt and pepper. Generously spread the mustard evenly over the beef, then top each piece with 2 bacon slices. In the center, arrange the slices from 1 pickle. Tightly roll the meat to form a roulade and secure by inserting skewers into both ends of the roll.

2. Place a medium saucepan or stew pot over medium heat and add the vegetable oil. When the oil is hot, add the rinderroulade and sear on all sides, about 2 minutes per side. Remove the meat from the pan and set aside.

3. Add the chopped onion to the pan and cook over medium heat for 5 minutes to soften. Then stir in the garlic and tomato paste and cook for 1 minute, until fragrant. Deglaze the pan with the red wine, scraping the pan bottom and letting the wine reduce for 1 minute. Add the beef stock, bay leaf, and seared rinderroulade. Reduce heat and bring the liquid to a simmer, then cover and cook for 1½ hours.

4. Test the doneness of the meat with a fork to make sure it's tender, remove it from the pan onto a serving platter, cover, and set aside. To form a rich, silky sauce, mix the contents of the cooking pan in a blender. Return to the stovetop and cook, stirring, until the gravy reaches the desired thickness. (For a thicker gravy, add either cornstarch or flour.) Stir in the butter and season to taste with salt and pepper.

5. Remove the skewers from the rinderroulade and serve smothered in the gravy.

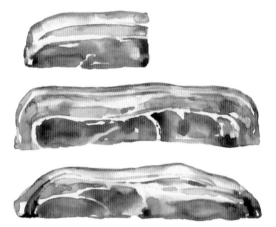

SAUERBRATEN

They say that time heals all wounds. This is not true—time does not heal samurai sword wounds. Those never heal. But one thing that time can always heal is tough cuts of meat, such as bottom round or rump roast. By marinating the meat for up to 10 days in a mixture of vinegar or wine, you'll transform leathery meat into something soft and tender. As we say in the Schrute family, "May your meat be tender and your heart sinewy." Enjoy.

Serves 4 ⏐ Prep time: 15 minutes, plus 2 to 3 days to marinate ⏐ Cook time: 3 hours, 10 minutes

1 large onion, roughly chopped

1 carrot, peeled and roughly chopped

1 leek, roughly chopped

3 cloves garlic

½ bunch fresh rosemary

2 bay leaves

2 cups dry red wine

2 cups beef stock

1 cup red wine vinegar

1 cup apple cider vinegar

1 teaspoon whole cloves

1 teaspoon juniper berries

1 teaspoon mustard seeds

1 teaspoon black peppercorns

1 teaspoon salt, plus more as desired

3 pounds beef chuck, roasting joint

1 tablespoon vegetable oil

1 tablespoon brown sugar

5 ounces (⅝ cup) crushed gingersnaps

½ cup golden raisins (optional)

salt and pepper, to taste

1. In a large saucepan or Dutch oven, combine the onion, carrot, leek, garlic, rosemary, bay leaves, red wine, beef stock, vinegars, cloves, juniper berries, mustard seeds, peppercorns, and 1 teaspoon of salt. Set over medium heat and bring the marinade mixture to a boil. Reduce to a simmer and cook for 10 minutes. Remove the pan from the stovetop and allow the contents to cool completely.

2. While the marinade cools, sear the beef chuck. Place a roasting pot over high heat and let it become very hot. Rub the vegetable oil over the beef and season generously with salt. Place the meat in the pot and sear, turning until well browned on all sides.

3. Transfer the seared beef into the cooled marinade, making sure it is completely submerged. Place the lid on the pot and marinate the beef in the refrigerator for 2 or 3 days.

4. When the meat has marinated, preheat the oven to 325°F. Cover the pot, place it in the oven, and roast the meat for 3 hours, until tender.

5. Remove the meat from the pot and set aside on a cutting board to rest. Strain the pot contents into a medium saucepan, discarding the solids. Place over medium heat and stir in the brown sugar, crushed gingersnaps, and raisins, if using. Simmer until thickened and season with salt and pepper to taste.

6. Cut the beef chuck into slices and serve on a platter, covered with the sweet and tangy gravy.

KARTOFFELKLOESSE

Some ignoramuses would have you believe that these potato dumplings originated in Norway. You know what we say to that? Lies! Potato dumplings were invented in the northern marshlands of medieval Bavaria. And what's more, these delicious kartoffelkloesse are topped with butter-fried breadcrumbs. Suck on those breadcrumbs, Norway.

Serves 4 ⫙ Prep time: 15 minutes ⫙ Cook time: 45 minutes

2 pounds russet potatoes

½ teaspoon salt, plus more for cooking water and seasoning

4 tablespoons (2 ounces) unsalted butter

½ cup bread cubes

1 cup all-purpose flour

2 eggs, lightly beaten

1. Place the potatoes in a medium saucepan, cover with water, and add ½ teaspoon of salt. Set over medium heat and bring to a simmer; cook for 15 to 20 minutes or until tender. Remove from the heat, pour out the liquid, and let the potatoes cool for 5 minutes. Peel while still warm and then mash smooth by hand or with an electric mixer. Transfer to a container and refrigerate until completely cooled.

2. Set a small sauté pan over medium heat and add the butter. Once the butter has melted, stir in the bread cubes and toast until crispy golden brown; set aside.

3. When the mashed potatoes have cooled, mix in the flour and eggs. Bring together into a uniform dough. Then divide into 12 portions, insert a buttered bread cube into the center of the dumplings, and roll into tight balls.

4. Place a large saucepan over medium heat and fill with water. Bring to a boil and add the dumplings. Simmer for 10 minutes, until the dumplings have risen to the top. Using slotted spoon, remove the dumplings and place on a serving platter. Pour the remaining butter and breadcrumb mixture over the dumplings to serve.

WOODCHUCK IN WINE

Would we ever trust a groundhog to be good at anything other than tasting delicious? Absolutely not. But it's just like Americans to rely on animals to do their bidding, like predicting the weather. Luckily, the Schrutes have a delicious use for this varmint that doesn't include seeing its shadow in February. This stew is tasty served with boiled potatoes, rice, or egg noodles.

Serves 4 | Prep time: 10 minutes | Cook time: 1 hour, 15 minutes

3 tablespoons olive oil

1 woodchuck (groundhog), cleaned, boned, and cut into strips

1 medium yellow onion, chopped

2 carrots, peeled and diced

1 clove garlic, minced

1 cup beef stock

2 cups dry red wine

¾ cup plus 2 tablespoons white vermouth

¼ teaspoon dried thyme

1 bay leaf

2 teaspoons black pepper

2 tablespoons chopped fresh rosemary, divided

1½ cups roughly chopped pitted Kalamata olives

2 to 3 tablespoons all-purpose flour

1 bunch fresh flat-leaf parsley, chopped

salt, as needed

1. Heat a Dutch oven or large, heavy pot over moderate to high heat for 1 minute. Add the olive oil and heat for 30 seconds, then add the woodchuck and brown on all sides. Transfer to a dish and set aside.

2. Add the chopped onion and carrots to the pot and lightly brown. Stir in the garlic and cook for 1 minute.

3. Add the beef stock, wine, and ¾ cup of vermouth, stirring with a wooden spoon. Be sure to scrape the stuck-on bits from the bottom of the pan—they have plenty of flavor.

4. Place the woodchuck meat back in the pot. Add the thyme, bay leaf, pepper, and half the rosemary.

5. Cover the pot, turn the heat down to low, and simmer for 20 minutes. Stir in the olives and remaining rosemary. Cover and simmer for 45 more minutes or until the meat is tender, stirring occasionally.

6. Discard the bay leaf. Turn the heat up, cover, and boil the stew for 10 minutes or until the liquid is reduced a little. In a small bowl, stir the remaining 2 tablespoons of vermouth with as much flour as needed to make a thin paste. Add this to the stew a tablespoon at a time, simmering for 1 minute after each addition. When the stew reaches the consistency you want, stir in the parsley; taste and add salt if needed.

BEET THIS

"EXOTIC" MEAT PIE

Want to impress an important guest on the summer solstice? Of course you do! Try this ancient Schrute family strategy: lying. Make this totally regular goat pie, but tell your guests it's their favorite exotic meat—such as giraffe, hippopotamus, manticore—or vegetarian. This trick can be used to turn enemies into friends, friends into lovers, or lovers into enemies. Enjoy!

Serves 3 ⁜ Prep time: 40 minutes ⁜ Cook time: 45 minutes

PASTRY

¼ teaspoon salt

1 cup all-purpose flour

⅓ cup shortening

¼ teaspoon white vinegar

1 egg yolk

1 tablespoon cold water, or as needed

2 teaspoons olive oil

¾ pound beef top sirloin steak, cut in ½-inch cubes

1 tablespoon butter

1 small onion, chopped

½ cup peeled and shredded tart apple

1 small white potato, peeled and cut in ½-inch cubes

1 clove garlic, minced

2 teaspoons all-purpose flour

1½ teaspoons beef bouillon granules

1 teaspoon minced fresh parsley

⅛ teaspoon dried thyme

⅛ teaspoon celery seed

⅛ teaspoon dried dill

⅛ teaspoon black pepper

½ cup plus 2 teaspoons water

1 egg yolk

1. To make the pastry dough, put the salt and 1 cup of flour in a medium bowl and cut in the shortening until you have a crumbly mixture. Stir in the vinegar and 1 egg yolk and then add the water gradually, mixing with a fork, until the dough forms a ball. You can add another teaspoon or so of water if needed. Divide the dough into two portions, one slightly bigger than the other. Cover and refrigerate for 30 minutes.

2. While the dough rests, heat the oil in a medium skillet over medium-high heat and then add the beef cubes, turning to brown on all sides. Use a slotted spoon to remove the meat from the pan; set aside. Using the same skillet, add the butter and sauté the onion, apple, and potato for 3 minutes, stirring occasionally or until the onion is tender.

3. Now stir in the garlic and cook for another minute. Stir in the 2 teaspoons of flour until well mixed. Add the bouillon, the browned beef cubes, the remaining seasonings, and ½ cup of water. Bring

BEET THIS

to a boil, then reduce the heat and simmer for a couple of minutes or until thickened.

4. Preheat the oven to 375°F. Roll out the larger piece of dough to fit a 7-inch pie dish. Transfer the pastry to the pie dish and trim along the edges. Spoon in the beef mixture. Roll out the remaining dough piece to fit the top of the pie. Place over the filling, then trim, seal, and flute the edges. Cut a few slits in the top.

5. Beat the remaining egg yolk with 2 teaspoons of water and brush onto the pastry top. Bake for 35 minutes, or until the crust is golden brown. Cut in wedges and serve warm.

TROUT SCHNITZEL

Ninjas, the U.S. military, and chameleons all learned the art of camouflage from trout—the original masters of disguise. The regionally specific colors and patterning of trout skin provide them with camouflage that is unique to their surroundings. That fact has very little to do with this delicious dish, but you're smarter and more handsome for knowing it.

Serves 6 | Prep time: 20 minutes | Cook time: 40 minutes

6 skinless rainbow trout fillets

1 large egg

¼ cup water

½ cup all-purpose flour

1 cup unseasoned panko breadcrumbs

1 tablespoon salt

2 tablespoons butter, for frying

CREAM SAUCE

2 to 3 unsalted tablespoons butter

1 shallot, peeled and sliced

½ cup dry white wine

2 cups heavy cream

juice of ½ lemon

1 tablespoon chopped fresh thyme leaves

2 tablespoons drained capers

2 tablespoons whole grain mustard

salt and black pepper, to taste

1. To prepare the trout, in a small bowl whisk together the egg and water. Put the flour in a separate shallow bowl, then mix the breadcrumbs and salt in a third bowl. Dip each trout fillet first in the flour, then in the egg wash, and finally in the breadcrumbs, turning to coat all sides.

BEET THIS

2. Transfer the trout to a paper towel–lined plate and refrigerate for 10 minutes to help the breading stay on during cooking.

3. For the sauce, melt the butter in a small pan over low to moderate heat; add the shallot and sauté for 5 minutes, stirring occasionally. Pour in the white wine and cook until almost completely reduced. Add the cream, cook to reduce by half, and add the remaining sauce ingredients. Cook gently for another few minutes.

4. Meanwhile, heat a large skillet over moderate heat, then add 2 tablespoons of butter and let it melt. Cook the fish fillets in batches, frying them for a few minutes per side or until golden. Add more butter if necessary.

5. Serve the trout schnitzel with the cream sauce ladled over the top. Spätzle, egg noodles, or boiled potatoes make a good accompaniment.

BEET SPÄTZLE

Spätzle is a German form of pasta. This beet-brightened twist on spätzle is sure to bring ample amounts of oohing and aahing. But that's not all. The incorporation of citrus provides such a perfect counterbalance to the density of the spätzle that male and female diners alike will erupt in spasms of pure pleasure. Needless to say, this dish is only suitable for adult audiences in private settings.

Serves 4 | Prep time: 15 minutes | Cook time: 30 minutes

½ cup peeled and roughly chopped cooked beet

2 cups all-purpose flour

1 teaspoon salt, plus more for cooking water and seasoning

3 eggs, lightly beaten

½ cup whole milk

4 tablespoons (2 ounces) butter

¼ cup crumbled goat cheese

2 tablespoons pine nuts

¼ cup chopped fennel fronds/dill/chervil

black pepper, to taste

1. In a blender, mix the cooked beet on high speed until a smooth, thick purée forms. Pour into a small bowl and set aside.

2. In a medium bowl, combine the flour and 1 teaspoon of salt. Create a well in the center and pour in the eggs, milk, and beet purée. Whisk together to form a loose dough.

3. Set a large saucepan of salted water over high heat and bring to a boil. Then hold a spätzle maker or colander over the pan and push the batter through the holes into the boiling water. This can be done in stages; do not overfill the saucepan or the spätzle pieces will stick together. Cook for 2 minutes; the dumplings are ready once they float to the top. Lift out the cooked spätzle and place in a bowl of ice water, then repeat the process until all the dough has been cooked. Line a baking tray with a cloth and transfer the cooked spätzle onto the tray.

4. Place a medium sauté pan over medium heat and add the butter. Pour in the cooked spätzle and toss it through the butter for 2 minutes to coat well. Remove the pan from the heat and add the goat cheese, pine nuts, and fennel fronds. Fold through to warm everything, then season with salt and pepper to taste. Distribute onto 4 plates to serve as an appetizer or a light main course.

Cook's Note: If you have an aversion to pine nuts, replace them with finely chopped apple to provide crunch.

SWEETS

We didn't want to include any sweets or desserts in this book. Sweets are the third biggest threat to humanity, behind only alien invasion and forgiveness. Sadly, our editors informed us that Americans need desserts in their cookbooks, so we were obliged to follow the instructions of our professional superiors. Some of the following dishes are not entirely unhealthy when eaten in small portions.

MOIST CHOCOLATE-BEET CAKE

This chocolate cake contains beets and is not entirely unhealthy in small portions. It is especially good spread with cream cheese and poppy seeds. Alternatively, you can butter it or simply enjoy it as it is.

Serves 8 ⫙ Prep time: 30 minutes ⫙ Cook time: 40 minutes

½ pound beets, boiled, peeled, and chopped

pinch of salt

7 ounces chopped bittersweet or semisweet chocolate

¼ cup hot espresso or water

⅞ cup (7 ounces) butter, cubed, at room temperature

3 tablespoons unsweetened cocoa powder

1 cup all-purpose flour

1¼ teaspoons baking powder

5 large eggs, at room temperature

1 cup sugar

1. Grease an 8-inch springform pan and line the base with parchment paper. Preheat the oven to 350°F.

2. Purée the beets in a food processor along with a pinch of salt. Set aside.

3. Melt the chocolate in a large bowl set over a pan of barely simmering water, not stirring much. When it's almost completely melted, pour in the hot espresso or water and stir briefly. Add the butter and let the chunks melt without stirring.

4. Into a bowl, sift the cocoa powder, flour, and baking powder.

5. Remove the chocolate mixture from the heat and stir briefly to completely mix in the butter. Let sit for 5 minutes.

6. Separate the egg whites from the yolks. Lightly beat the yolks and stir them into the chocolate mixture. Fold in the beets as well.

7. Whip the egg whites until stiff, using a hand or stand mixer. Use a spatula to fold in the sugar, then carefully fold this mixture into the chocolate mixture. Now fold in the flour mixture.

8. Transfer the batter into the prepared cake pan and turn the oven temperature down to 325°F. Bake for 40 minutes, or until the center is still a little wobbly but the edges are just set. Let cool completely on a wire rack before removing from the pan.

Note: It's important not to overmix or overcook this cake. The ingredients should be just combined, and the cake should be just set at the edges when you take it out of the oven.

BEET PUDDING

This savory dessert has beets and is soft, making it an excellent choice for those with weak teeth. Ironically, beet pudding contains a moderate amount of calcium, which will strengthen your teeth. Then you will no longer need to eat beet pudding. But shortly after you stop eating beet pudding, you will become calcium deficient again. Beet pudding: one of life's vicious cycles.

Serves 8 ⸙ Prep time: 10 minutes ⸙ Cook time: 55 minutes

6 large beets, peeled and finely chopped

¼ cup lemon juice

1 teaspoon salt, plus more to taste

½ teaspoon sugar

⅓ cup (2.7 ounces) unsalted butter, plus more for baking dish

3 large eggs

BEET THIS

1¼ cups heavy cream

1 teaspoon chopped fresh tarragon leaves

black pepper, to taste

balsamic vinegar glaze (optional)

1. In a medium saucepan, combine the beets, lemon juice, 1 teaspoon of salt, sugar, and ⅓ cup of butter. Add water to just cover the beets and bring to a boil. Reduce the heat slightly and put a lid on the pan. Simmer for 30 minutes, adding more water if needed.

2. Turn the heat up and remove the lid. Boil the mixture, stirring constantly, until thick and syrupy. Remove from the heat and let cool for 10 minutes.

3. Preheat the oven to 350°F.

4. In a food processor, mix the eggs with the cream. Add the beet mixture and pulse a few times to blend. Mix in the tarragon, pepper, and more salt, if desired.

5. Grease a 9 x 9-inch baking dish with butter and fill with the beet mixture. Alternatively, you can use ramekins; fill each one to the lower rim.

6. Bake for about 25 minutes, or until a knife inserted in the middle comes out nearly clean.

7. Run a knife around the edges of the pudding to loosen it. Serve immediately, drizzled with a balsamic vinegar glaze if you wish.

GOOEY CHOCOLATE BEET COOKIES

These beet cookies just may take the cake. They are healthful, chewy, and robust, with just the slightest hint of charcoal and grit to overpower the sweetness of the chocolate. For a real winter treat, try dipping a beet cookie in a hot glassful of sweet, nutty horse milk. Don't like horse milk? Goat milk is a great alternative.

Makes about 18 cookies (depending on size)
Prep time: 10 minutes ⏐ Cook time: 15 minutes

1 cup all-purpose flour

½ teaspoon baking powder

¼ teaspoon salt

2 tablespoons sugar

½ cup finely shredded raw beets

¼ cup dark chocolate chips, or chips of your choice

2 tablespoons cooking oil

1. Preheat the oven to 400°F. Line a baking sheet with parchment paper.

2. In a medium bowl, whisk together the flour, baking powder, salt, and sugar. Add the shredded beets and chocolate chips, using your hands to mix them in thoroughly. Add the oil and combine everything, again using your hands, until you have a smooth dough.

3. Place the dough on parchment paper on a smooth surface and form into a flat disk, then roll to ½-inch thickness. Use a knife to cut the dough into squares, or use cookie cutters to make shapes. Transfer to the prepared baking sheet.

4. Bake for 15 minutes, or until set. Let the cookies cool on a rack, and then enjoy!

BEET CINNAMON BUNS

Orange zest, ginger, and cinnamon add the perfect pop to these sweet treats, while the subtle addition of the beets gives an enjoyably smooth finish. But be warned—these cinnamon buns are dangerously addictive. One young Schrute, for example, ate 47 of them in one sitting and had to be removed from his chair by forklift. What happened next? The Great Schrute Farms Forklift Accident led to the escape of more than ten thousand honeybees!

Makes 12 buns ⚬ Prep time: 2 hours, 30 minutes ⚬
Cook time: 15 minutes

DOUGH

½ cup plus 1 teaspoon sugar

¼ cup warm water, about 105°F

4½ teaspoons active dry yeast

1 cup mashed boiled beets

1 cup buttermilk

BEET THIS

1 egg, lightly beaten

4 tablespoons (2 ounces) unsalted butter, melted

1 tablespoon plus 1 teaspoon grated orange zest

1¼ teaspoons salt

3½ cups white whole wheat flour

2½ cups light spelt flour

1 egg whisked with 2 teaspoons water, for egg wash

1½ tablespoons brown sugar

FILLING

¾ cup brown sugar

1 tablespoon ground cinnamon

¼ teaspoon ground ginger

3 tablespoons softened unsalted butter, divided

1. In a stand mixer bowl, dissolve 1 teaspoon of sugar in the warm water. Sprinkle the yeast on top and let the mixture stand for 5 minutes, or until you see bubbles. Then add the beets, buttermilk, lightly beaten egg, melted butter, orange zest, salt, and remaining sugar. Mix together using the paddle attachment.

2. Add half the whole wheat and spelt flours and continue to mix. Swap the paddle attachment for a dough hook attachment. Add the remaining flours and knead for 5 minutes, or until the dough makes a ball.

3. Transfer the dough to a lightly greased medium bowl; cover and leave to rise at room temperature for at least 1½ hours. Alternatively, you can put it in the refrigerator overnight and then let it come back to room temperature.

4. For the filling, in a small bowl, mix the ¾ cup brown sugar with the ginger and cinnamon.

5. Divide the dough in half. On a floured surface, roll each portion into a 20 x 13-inch rectangle. Spread 3 tablespoons of butter over each rectangle. Sprinkle the ginger and cinnamon mixture on top, leaving a ½-inch border all around.

6. Roll the dough up into tight logs, then pinch the seams closed and set the logs seam side down. Slice each dough log into 12 pieces, cutting on the diagonal. Press the top and center of each piece to help shape it.

7. Line a pair of baking sheets with parchment paper and arrange the rolls 2 inches apart on the paper. Cover with plastic wrap and let rise for 30 minutes.

8. Preheat the oven to 400°F. Brush the egg wash over the top of each roll and sprinkle with the 1½ tablespoons brown sugar. Bake for 15 minutes, or until golden. Serve warm.

Note: Leftover rolls can be wrapped in foil and frozen, then reheated in the oven.

RED VELVET CUPCAKES

Cupcakes with veggies? Of course! These ingenious cups of cake use beets instead of food coloring, resulting in a rich crimson hue as opposed to a sinister, unnatural red. Delicious, vegetable, color. That's three strikes. Touchdown!

Makes 24 cupcakes 🍴 Prep time: 25 minutes 🍴
Cook time: 16 minutes

10 ounces beets

2 tablespoons lemon juice

¾ cup buttermilk

¾ cup canola oil

4 large eggs

2½ cups all-purpose flour

3 tablespoons unsweetened cocoa powder

1½ cups sugar

2 teaspoons baking powder

½ teaspoon baking soda

1 teaspoon salt

4 tablespoons (2 ounces) unsalted butter, softened

1 (8-ounce) package cream cheese, softened

1 pound (3½ cups) powdered sugar

1 teaspoon vanilla extract

1 cup chopped, toasted walnuts or pecans (optional)

1. Preheat the oven to 350°F. Scrub the beets, then wrap each one in parchment paper. Twist to seal. Microwave on high for 8 minutes, or until tender, then let rest until cool enough to handle.

2. Peel and roughly chop the beets, then process in a food processor with the lemon juice. Add the buttermilk and oil and process, then add the eggs and process again until smooth.

3. Whisk together the flour, cocoa, sugar, baking powder, baking soda, and salt. Add the beet mixture and whisk to just combine. Line 24 muffin cups with baking liners, then fill each ⅔ full with the cake batter.

4. Bake for 16 minutes, or until a toothpick inserted into the center of a cupcake comes out clean. Set the muffin cups on a cooling rack for half an hour.

5. Meanwhile, use a handheld or stand mixer to beat the butter and cream cheese until smooth. Add the powdered sugar gradually, beating at low speed until the frosting is light, fluffy, and well blended. Beat in the vanilla extract.

6. Spread the frosting over the cupcakes using an offset spatula, or use a zip-top plastic bag with a snipped-off corner to pipe it on decoratively. Sprinkle with walnuts or pecans, if you wish.

BEET THIS

DRINKS

Alcohol has been consumed since at least 13,000 BC, when some enterprising cavemen turned their caves into breweries. But the pinnacle of alcohol manufacturing wasn't reached until the beet was introduced to the fermentation process. Odorless, colorless, and as smooth as a newborn weasel, beet alcohol is the perfect base for home brewing and distillation. Read on for step-by-step instructions for everything from beet beer and wine to classic Schrute cocktails made from our local award-winning beet vodka. *Prost.*

GRANDMOTHER GERTRUDE'S BEET WINE

Northeastern Pennsylvania is often compared favorably to California's Napa Valley because of the abundance of award-winning beet wines it produces. Beet wine has a muscular, mulchy taste, with undertones of organic manure, gravel, and unripe wild strawberry. The leathery finish is out of this world. Beet wine is also far superior to grape-based wines in that it takes only 4 to 6 months to ferment into a robust and mature *rübenwein*.

Makes 1 gallon ⚊ Prep time: 30 to 45 minutes ⚊
Fermentation time: 1 month ⚊ Age time: 4 to 6 months

5 pounds beets, unpeeled, sliced into thin pieces

1 gallon water, or more as needed

2¼ cups raisins, diced

10 cups sugar

1 cup uncooked rice

⅓ tablespoon dry yeast

1. In a large pot, cover the beets with water and boil until the slices are tender. Transfer the beet slices and liquid into a large jar for fermenting, adding water until you have 1 gallon of liquid.

2. In a medium bowl, mix the raisins with the sugar, rice, and yeast. Pour into the jar with the beets.

3. The beet wine will take a month to fully ferment; make sure you stir it daily during the fermentation process. Once the wine is fermented, siphon it into sterile wine bottles, seal, and cork. Then age your beet wine for 4 to 6 months before enjoying.

UNCLE BERT'S BEET BEER

An adventurous alternative to regular beer, Uncle Bert's Beet Beer is world famous in Lancaster, Pennsylvania. It has won several awards, including "Western Pennsylvania's Fourteenth Best Beet Beer" in 1927 and "Honorary Mention" in 2016's Best of Craft Beer Awards. Beet beers are famous for their bright crimson hues and robust finish. The inclusion of beets in the mash brings an earthen flavor to what would otherwise be far too fruity and peppery. This beer pairs well with a nice wheel of your favorite moose cheese. For home brewing, you'll need a brew kettle.

Makes 1 to 2 gallons ⫲ Prep time: 3 hours ⫲
Fermentation time: 7 to 14 days ⫲ Age time: 14 days

6 medium beets, 4 for mash and 2 for final flavor

4 gallons distilled water, plus more as needed

4 pounds Pilsner malt

½ pound caramel malt

½ pound aromatic malt

¼ pound honey malt

2 ounces hops (Fuggle, Willamette, or Styrian Savinjski Golding)

pinch of Irish moss

3 pounds dry malt extract

1 pack Belle Saison dry yeast

⅔ cup corn sugar, for priming

2 cups (16-ounces) water, for priming

1. Wash, peel, and wrap 4 beets in aluminum foil and roast in a preheated 400°F oven for 1 hour.

2. Heat 4 gallons of water to 150°F in your brew kettle.

BEET THIS

3. Combine the cooked beets and malt grains (for mash) for 1 hour in the kettle. Once your grains are sparged (or have been rinsed of all remaining sugars) remove the grains and beets and discard. Bring what remains to a boil, add the hops and Irish moss, and boil for 1 hour. Turn off the heat and dissolve the malt extract in the boiled liquid. Cool the wort (liquid) with a wort chiller or place in a sink with cold water and use cold, distilled water to top off to 5 gallons.

4. Pitch the yeast (add to the chilled wort) and allow the solution to ferment at room temperature for 7 days. If your hydrometer shows a gravity of around 1.010, rack the beer (transfer off the yeast to another vessel) for another 7 days.

5. Add corn sugar and water to a medium saucepan and bring to a boil. Once it cools, add it to your bottling container/bucket.

6. Finally, for a handsome beet flavor and color, boil 2 medium peeled beets, cool the pot to room temperature, and toss the boiled beet mixture into your secondary fermenter. Bottle your final solution and let age at room temperature for 14 days.

BEET VODKA

Question: Who invented vodka? The Russians. Question: Where do beets come from? Somewhere in the Mediterranean. Final question: Whose idea was it to have these two form an alliance? America's. *Perfectenschlag*.

Makes 1 to 2 gallons ⧚ Prep time: 2 hours ⧚
Fermentation time: 14 to 17 days

MASH

30 pounds beets, boiled, peeled, and roughly chopped

5 gallons filtered water or as needed

malt or amylase enzyme powder

mash pot

sugar (optional)

1. Mash the beets by hand or with an immersion blender. Transfer to your mash pot and add enough water to make 5 gallons.

2. Add the malt or amylase to the beets to help break down the starches into sugar. Heat at 150°F for at least 1 hour, covered; stir periodically. Take a gravity reading. If it is below 1.070, add enough sugar to reach 1.070. Let cool to room temperature.

BEET THIS

hydrometer	1 package distiller's yeast
mason jar	fermentation bucket
½ cup water	airlock
2 tablespoons fermenting sugar solution	cheesecloth

3. Create a yeast starter. Grab a sanitized mason jar and pour in water at 110°F. Add fermenting sugar to the water; stir thoroughly. Add the distiller's yeast and stir thoroughly. Let this solution sit uncovered for 20 minutes; it should double in volume. Then transfer the mash liquid to the fermentation bucket. To retrieve the liquid, pour the mash through a strainer. Tip: Try to create as much splash as you can to help aerate the mixture.

4. Add the airlock and ferment the mixture for up to 2 weeks at room temperature. When bubbling has stopped in the fermentation bucket, wait 2 or 3 days and then take the final gravity reading to calculate the alcohol by volume. Strain the fermentation mixture through cheesecloth to remove any solid material; discard the solids. (Note: the solids can cause headaches if kept around too long, so make sure to quickly dispose.)

DISTILLATION

column still	copper column packing

5. Add copper packing to your column still. Add your fermentation mixture (also known as the wash) to the still. Make sure that you've separated any remaining solids from the liquor (see previous step).

6. Connect the column to the boiler and attach a cooling hose, making sure everything is properly connected. Turn on the heat and raise the temperature of the wash to approximately 170°F. This is when the still will start producing. You'll want to throw out the first 35 percent of your run, which is equivalent to ⅓ of a pint jar (this includes the foreshots and the heads, which are toxic and can be fatal). The next 30 percent will be the sweet spot— the "hearts" that you will want to keep. The last 35 percent, the tails, cannot be consumed and should be thrown out because they contain chemicals.

7. Bottle your vodka and store in a safe, dry place. You can use your beet vodka to make delicious cocktails. Enjoy.

> **How to Calculate Alcohol by Volume (ABV)**
> Subtract the original gravity (OG) from the final gravity (FG). Multiply this number by 131.25 to get the alcohol percentage, the ABV.
>
> A good wash for vodka is between 7 and 10 percent ABV.

BEET THIS

THE AMERICA

The America is similar to the Bloody Mary, but much more patriotic. Because of its colors. The beverage itself is Old Glory Red (the second-best red), while the garnishes of Albino beet and blue potato are white and Old Glory Blue, respectively. As an option, you can add American meats to the garnish. Consider a hamburger, a prized strip of jerky, or a hot dog.

Serves 1 ⦙ Prep time: 2 minutes

2 ounces (¼ cup) Beet Vodka (see page 136)

4 ounces (½ cup) tomato juice

1 dash Worcestershire sauce

1 dash hot sauce

½ teaspoon prepared horseradish

½ teaspoon fresh-ground black pepper

1½ teaspoons lime juice

1 tablespoon lemon juice

1 slice Albino beet, for garnish

1 slice roasted blue potato, for garnish

Add everything except the beet and potato slices to a shaker filled with ice. Stir and then strain into a highball glass. Garnish with beet and potato slices.

THE IRRIGATION

This classic beet-vodka cocktail celebrates irrigation, the second best use of water. (The first best use of water is rain on your enemy's wedding day.) It combines beet vodka, triple sec, and fresh lime for a bright summer treat. Add in a dash of water from your favorite well, and *prost!* It's irrigation party time!

Serves 1 ⏐ Prep time: 2 minutes

2 ounces (¼ cup) Beet Vodka (see page 136)

1 ounce (⅛ cup) lime juice

1 ounce (⅛ cup) triple sec

lime wedge, for garnish

Fill a cocktail shaker with ice and add the vodka, lime juice, and triple sec. Shake well and strain into a chilled martini glass. Garnish with a lime wedge.

BEET THIS

NIGHTTIME

Nighttime is a beet vodka cocktail that celebrates nighttime—the time of day that is both the scariest and the most sensual. The Nighttime is similar to a Black Russian but also different. It's better. It has beets. Caffeine, alcohol, and beets—the three perfect ingredients for an unforgettable all-night Rumspringa! Hurrah!

Serves 1 ⎮ Prep time: 2 minutes

2 ounces (¼ cup) Kahlúa coffee liqueur

1 ounce (⅛ cup) Beet Vodka (see page 136)

Pour the Kahlúa and vodka into a mixing glass filled with ice. Stir, then pour through a strainer over fresh ice in a rocks glass.

THE SCRANTON:
THE REAL ORIGINAL
MANHATTAN

Fact: The Manhattan was invented at the Manhattan Club in Manhattan, New York, by Dr. Iain Marshall in 1875. FALSE! The Manhattan was actually invented right here in Pennsylvania in 1854 by one Mrs. Gilda Schrute (better known as Great Grandmother Schrute). Within a decade, this cocktail had proliferated in the illicit stills of Susquehannock State Forest. By the early 1880s, it had spread eastward to New York City. One year later, Dr. Marshall "introduced" it to the world. Yes, Dr. Marshall popularized the Manhattan. But Great Grandmother Schrute created it.

Serves 1 | Prep time: 2 minutes

2 ounces (¼ cup) whiskey

1 ounce (⅛ cup) sweet vermouth

2 dashes bitters

beet peel, for garnish

whole miniature beets, for garnish

Fill a cocktail shaker with ice. Add the whiskey, vermouth, and bitters; stir. Strain into a martini glass over a single large ice cube. Rub the beet peel over the rim of the glass for an earthen taste, then garnish with the beet peel and plop in a few runt beets.

BEET THIS

ABOUT THE AUTHORS

Tyanni Niles is a writer, crafter, and former instrumentalist. T.Y.A.N.N.I. stands for Talented. Youthful. Awesome. Natural-born warrior. Nifty. Important. In a past life, she was a martial artist, made obvious to her because she strongly relates to a number of anime characters. Her previous sensei made her consume hundreds of beets at a time and binge on hundreds of *The Office* episodes as part of her training. Because of this, she now has the power of five Super Saiyans combined.

Sam Kaplan is a humorist, therapist, and former professional gardener. His ancestors were time travelers, brewers, vampire hunters, and lentil farmers. Sam has several special skills, including the ability to grow or shrink an inch throughout the day. He claims this is because he has consumed nearly 100,000 beets in his lifetime and given nearly twice that many high fives. According to recent analysis, he has the strength of a juvenile hippopotamus.

Keith Riegert has applied for the position of Assistant Regional Manager at Cumberland Mills and is still waiting to hear back. In his spare time, Keith is an acclaimed amateur taxidermist, having won second place in the distinguished Westmoreland County Biannual Pennsylvania Native Fauna Full Body Mount taxidermy competition. He lives alone.